NEW YORK STATE GRADE 6

ENGLISH LANGUAGE ARTS TEST

Cynthia A. Lassonde, Ph.D.
SUNY College at Oneonta

BARRON'S

DEDICATION

To the students using this book.
I hope reading and writing
become your lifelong friends.
—CL

Photo credits: Unless otherwise indicated, all photos have been supplied by **Shutterstock.**

All inquiries should be addressed to:
Barron's Educational Series, Inc.
250 Wireless Blvd.
Hauppauge, NY 11788
www.barronseduc.com

ISBN-13: 978-0-7641-4030-3
ISBN-10: 0-7641-4030-2

Library of Congress Catalog Card No. 2008017021

Library of Congress Cataloging-in-Publication Data

Lassonde, Cynthia A.
    New York State grade 6 intermediate-level English language arts test / Cynthia A. Lassonde.
        p. cm.
    Includes index.
    ISBN-13: 978-0-7641-4030-3
    ISBN-10: 0-7641-4030-2
    1. Language arts (Middle school)—Ability testing—New York (State)—New York.
I. Title.

    LB1631.5.L37 2008
    372.6076—dc22

                                                    2008017021

Printed in the United States of America

9 8 7 6 5 4 3

CONTENTS

INTRODUCTION

THE NEW YORK STATE ENGLISH LANGUAGE ARTS LEARNING STANDARDS

What are State Standards? Standards outline the skills and knowledge all students in prekindergarten through Grade 12 must attain. They are a result of the nation's concern that all children reach certain expectations. The New York State Standards were originally written in the mid-1990s. They are published by the New York State Department of Education. Chapter 2 provides a full description of the English Language Arts (ELA) Standards and their purpose.

THE MISSION OF THE TESTING PROGRAM

The New York State tests are designed to check that students are learning the State Learning Standards. To meet the No Child Left Behind requirements, State English Language Arts tests are given annually in Grades 3 through 8. The tests measure student progress to ensure they are meeting grade-level criteria. They are not used, however, as the only measurement for students moving on to the next grade. That means students will not be retained in a grade because they did poorly on these State tests. The tests are good indicators, though, to see if students need extra help. The tests might also be helpful in acquiring extra training and assistance for teachers and school districts.

HOW TO USE THIS BOOK

This *New York State Grade 6 English Language Arts Test* manual is not only a test preparation guide but also a handbook of effective reading, writing, listening, and test-taking strategies. The information and practice tests provided within the pages of this guide aim to help students develop valuable and efficient strategies they will use across content areas and into their high-school years. By becoming proficient with the strategies presented in this book, students will become confident test takers who enter the classroom equipped with the literacy skills required to do well on the Grade 6 English Language Arts test.

The guide begins by introducing the ELA Standards and giving a little of the background of the evolution of the testing program. The purpose of this is to provide students with an understanding of the value of doing their best on the tests. It has been my experience as a fifth- and sixth-grade teacher for more than a decade that when students know why they are being asked to learn something and they can apply it to their lives in practical ways, they are more engaged, interested, and motivated to participate.

Chapter 1 describes and teaches what good readers, writers, and listeners do to be successful at comprehending what they have read and heard and at expressing what they understand through writing. Specific test-taking strategies will also be described. By presenting scientifically based, research-proven strategies that have been shown to be beneficial in promoting students' literacy skills, this chapter provides a firm foundation for students as they learn to apply these strategies in the following chapters and to the Grade 6 ELA test.

Chapter 2 provides an overview of the test. Students will learn what the test is composed of: the types of questions, the testing schedule, and the parts of the test. They will also learn how they will be expected to respond; the responsibilities of the school, their teacher, and themselves; and how their responses will be scored. By learning about the test, they will know what to expect and how to best prepare.

Chapters 3, 4, and 5 look separately at each of the three books that make up the test. These chapters are formatted in a similar sequence so students become familiar and comfortable with their contents. Basically, students will learn about the contents of each book, they will learn and practice strategies for completing that part of the test, and then they will practice the strategies they have learned in sample test questions. Following the samples, answers are provided with explanations for each. A think-aloud approach is used that talks the student through the thinking process used to successfully answer the questions. Possible helpful strategies are explained.

Chapters 6 and 7 contain two complete practice tests. Answers and explanations are provided, too.

The appendices include descriptions of literary genres, a glossary of terms students should know, and sample scoring rubrics for the short and extended written responses. Throughout the book, important terms are highlighted in blue the first time they are used to indicate these terms are explained more fully in the glossary.

A FINAL WORD

Do you want to improve your reading, writing, and listening skills? Do you want to do well on the State tests? Then you are on your way. Being motivated and eager to do your best is probably the most important factor in doing well. By studying and putting effort into doing the practice exercises in this book, you are taking advantage of this opportunity to improve your literacy skills and to learn new strategies for reading, writing, and listening. These strategies and practice will help you do your best on the Grade 6 ELA State tests as you improve your skills. Good luck!

BECOMING AN EFFECTIVE READER, WRITER, AND LISTENER

WHAT IS LITERACY?

The New York State Grade 6 English Language Arts (ELA) test assesses your literacy skills. But, what is literacy? Literacy involves being able to communicate with others through reading, writing, listening, and speaking. We are literate if we can understand others and they can understand us. There are lots of ways to be literate. You can be computer literate and know how to get around on the Internet. You are literate on the job if you can read instruction manuals and communicate with your coworkers.

In school we read, write, listen, and speak all the time and for lots of purposes. We read books, watch videos, use computers, write journals, present oral reports, and complete group projects.

Literacy is more than just something you do in school, though. Think of all the ways you read and write outside of school and school assignments. Do you do any of the following?

- Read or write just for pleasure? (Favorite magazines count!)
- Search the Internet?
- E-mail or chat online?
- Blog or use MySpace?
- Use automotive or other kinds of manuals?

✓ ■ Talk with friends about your favorite television shows and movies?

✓ ■ Listen to and enjoy music and lyrics or other creative arts?

✓ ■ Complete sudoku or crossword puzzles?

These are all examples of literacy. They involve creating meaning from texts that we read and listen to and expressing ourselves through writing. The more we practice our literacy skills inside and outside school, the better we become at them. Practice makes perfect! (Or at least it makes us better at doing something.) When we are interested in and excited about engaging in literacy activities, like the ones listed, we get better by trying new things and experimenting.

WHY DO I NEED LITERACY SKILLS?

Believe it or not, the more effort you put into becoming a really good reader, writer, and listener, the better prepared you will be to do well as a student, a worker, a parent, and a member of your community. Maybe that seems like a long way off right now. And it is! But now is the time to learn these skills so that you can build on them throughout your lifetime.

With that said, then, what does it mean to be a good reader, writer, and listener? Let's start by looking at the strategies we know good readers use when they read.

WHAT ARE SOME EFFECTIVE LITERACY STRATEGIES?

Good readers, writers, and listeners practice certain habits. They use strategies or methods that help them understand and help them express what they know. They pay attention and read closely and carefully. They don't just read the words and let their minds go blank. They keep their minds awake and active so they can absorb and think about what is going on. They enter the world of the story and almost become one of the characters. When they write, they do the same. They not only think about the message they want to get across in their writing, but they also read what they have written as if they were a stranger who just happened to come along. They think like a writer, but they also think like their readers. And, of course, good listeners do the same. They pay close attention to the speaker and don't let their minds wander or become distracted.

Here are some effective strategies. You probably use many of them already! But which ones should you try out? Which ones will help you improve your literacy skills?

READING STRATEGIES

Here are some reading strategies good readers use. Check off how often you use these strategies when you read—always, sometimes, or never. Then, try using each of them—especially the ones you don't ordinarily use—in reading the sample passage that follows. Note which strategies you find the most useful.

Before reading something, do you...

Always	Sometimes	Never	
____	✓ ____	____	Look over the title, any headings, pictures, and captions to get an idea of what the piece is about?
____	____	✓ ____	Skim through the piece to see how it is organized and how long it is?
✓ ____	____	____	Think about what you already know or have read about the topic?
✓ ____	____	____	Predict what you might learn from the piece or what the story might be about?

While reading something, do you...

Always	Sometimes	Never	
_____	✓	_____	Make the words and the story come alive by creating a movie in your mind? Visualize the characters and events? Ask yourself, Have I entered the world of the story?
_____	✓	_____	Ask yourself, Do I still understand what is going on here?
_____	✓	_____	Go back and reread from the place where you did understand to figure out what you missed the first time through?
_____	✓	_____	Ask yourself, What safe predictions can I make about what is going to happen next?
_____	✓	_____	Use clues from the piece to figure out vocabulary words you do not know?

After reading something, do you...

Always	Sometimes	Never	
_____	✓	_____	Think about the really important ideas and how they are connected with each other?
✓	_____	_____	Try to figure out the main idea or purpose of the piece?
_____	✓	_____	Try to "read between the lines" or think about possible hidden meanings or messages?
✓	_____	_____	Figure out your feelings about the piece? Ask yourself, Did I like it or not? Why? Did it make me laugh or feel sad? Was it realistic and logical?
_____	✓	_____	Ask yourself, How does this connect with what I already knew about the topic? How does it differ from or add to what I already knew?
✓	_____	_____	Summarize the piece in your own words?

SAMPLE READING PASSAGE

Read the following story about an imaginary place called Axel City. As you read, practice the strategies in the boxes and respond to the questions. Possible answers are listed below. You probably never realized you do so much when you read!

---

1. Before reading: Look over the title, any headings, pictures, and captions. What do they tell you?

   They tell me dhat it is about an ideapark and a skating paradise.

2. Before reading: Skim through the piece to see how it is organized and how long it is. What does this tell you?

   This tells me that is isn't that structured long and it is organized on so what it is, where it is, when it is, and how it is.

3. Before reading: What do you already know or what have you read about the topic?

   Not much, but I do know that it is imaginary

4. Before reading: Predict. What might you learn from the piece? What might the story be about?

   It might be about something called Axel city and it is a skate park I will learn about when it was

discovered.

A FIGURE SKATER'S PARADISE

Aubrey Adams

© Ruta Saulyte-Laurinaviciene

Introduction

Axel City, New York, came together out of a brilliant plan created by a group of professional figure skaters, coaches, seamstresses, and others. These people came together to construct a blueprint of how the city was to be developed. Then they hired an urban planner who designed how the city would be built.

> 5. While reading: Use clues from the piece to figure out vocabulary words. What is an urban planner?
>
> Someone who plans buildings in urban environments

Axel City was founded June 21, 2007, as a way to experiment with creative urban planning and to celebrate the graceful sport of figure skating. Since the city's theme is ice skating, there are several streets, hotels, and shops named after professionals in the field, skating moves, and other aspects of the culture. Figure skating is a way of life in Axel City. This city is a figure skater's paradise.

6. While reading: Do you understand what is going on?

Yes.

_____

_____

If not, go back and reread.

7. While reading: Create a movie in your mind. What do you think the city looks like? Sketch it here based on the description.

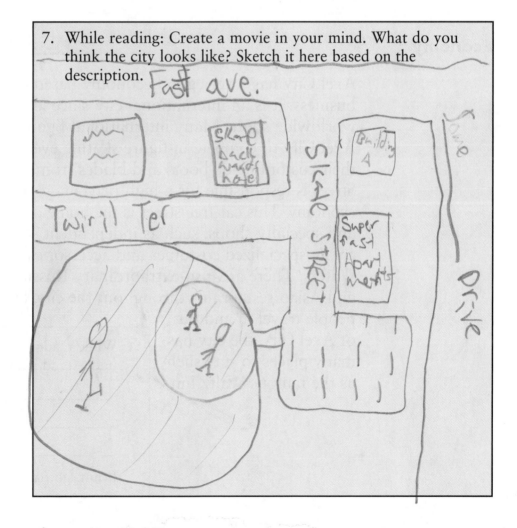

Organizational Structure

The center of Axel City contains a world famous ice rink called The Loop. This rink is famous for being the largest ice rink in the world. Surrounding the rink there are factories that custom-make boots and blades for skaters. The main street, Salchow Street, runs from one end of the city to the other. Salchow Street, named after a difficult skating jump, is the home of companies that design skating costumes in an array of colors and styles. Additionally, there are hotels, such as the Waltz Inn, shops for skating apparel, and much more.

> 8. While reading: Ask yourself, What safe predictions can I make about what is going to happen in this section?
>
> *Lots of aqructions will be based on skating.*

Economy

Axel City has a very good economy based on tourism and business. It is an international city since ice skating is a worldwide sport. Many international figure skaters come to Axel City to compete in figure skating events. They order their custom-made boots and blades from the city. Salchow Street is responsible for a high percentage of the city's economy. This car-free street is the home of many businesses and specialty shops, such as independent seamstresses who create specialized costumes and accessories for figure skaters. There are also extraordinary Russian, Canadian, and Asian restaurants throughout the city. Since many people travel in and out of Axel City, the city has many places to stay such as the famous Waltz Inn.

> 9. While reading: Do you understand what is going on?
>
> *Yes.*
>
> If not, go back and reread.

Conclusion

Axel City is an experiment in creative urban planning. It is the only figure skating city like it in the world. There are several distinct neighborhoods, hotels, shops, rinks, and roads that strengthen the skating theme of this city. Axel City is a unique place to visit and live. But don't forget to bring your skates!

AFTER READING

10. What do you think the main idea or purpose of the piece is?

All about Axel city

11. What possible hidden meanings or messages can be read between the lines?

None.

12. What are your feelings about the piece?

It's okay.

13. How does this piece connect with what you already knew about the topic?

I didn't know anything about the topic.

14. How does it differ from or how does it add to what you already knew?

It doesn't

15. How would you summarize the piece in your own words?

It is about an imaginary place called Axel city.

POSSIBLE ANSWERS

1. The piece is about a place that figure skaters would love. It will tell me about the structure and the economy of the place.

2. The piece isn't too long, and it has short paragraphs. So, it probably gives brief details about the place rather than complicated descriptions.

3. I like figure skating, and I've been to some shows. I know some of the well-known skaters' names. I do some figure skating myself for fun. I don't compete or anything, though.

4. I might learn about a place I could visit with my family. I want to know why it is such a paradise for figure skaters.

5. The paragraph talks about developing the city and the urban planner designing how the city would be built. So I think an urban planner designs cities.

6. I wasn't sure if the city was based on all kinds of skating or just figure skating, so I went back to the first paragraph and reread it. It sounds like it's based only on figure skating because it talks about seamstresses. I know figure skaters have fancy costumes.

7.

The Loop

seamstress	hotel	restaurant	apparel shop	hotel	hotel	shop
factory	shop	restaurant	shop	hotel	restaurant	factory

Salchow Street

8. This section is going to tell me about how people in the city make money.

9. Yes, I understand what is going on.

10. The main idea is that Axel City, New York, is a unique and thriving city based on a figure skating theme. I think the purpose of the piece is to inform the reader about the city.

11. I think the author is suggesting we should go there and check it out. I think the writer likes the city, too.

12. I liked the piece because I like ice skating. I don't think Axel City is a real place, though. I had never heard of it before this.

13. Knowing a little about figure skating helped me visualize what the ice rink and shops might look like.
14. The piece made me realize what a big business figure skating really is. There are lots of people, like seamstresses and coaches, who make a living from it.
15. Axel City, New York, is a theme city that is a paradise for figure skaters. The city is based on figure skating and is designed around an ice rink. The businesses make their income from tourists and competitors who come to the city, stay, and buy goods and services.

WRITING STRATEGIES

Now, the thing you have to remember about writing is that you are going to communicate your thoughts to someone. That can be a difficult thing to do. Sometimes we know what we mean to say, but we have a hard time writing it down in a clear, understandable way that other people can appreciate. When writing, we don't have a chance to talk with the reader face to face to explain what we mean when he gets confused. We have to do it through the words, sentences, and paragraphs that we write.

Before you write, really think through what you want to say. Plan your writing. Then when you write, your thoughts will become clearer. Therefore, your writing will be organized, and it will be easy for the reader to follow your train of thought. Also, when you write, don't be afraid to revise or change things around. The first time through, just draft your ideas. Then go back and think about organizing them more clearly. Group "like" things together.

Writing can be a messy process. Good writers don't just sit down and write from the beginning to the end of an article. They insert details, move paragraphs around to make more sense, and even scratch out whole parts if they stray off topic. Here are some strategies good writers practice. Which of them do you use always, sometimes, and never? Check them off. Then, practice using them by responding to the writing prompt that follows.

Before writing something, do you...

Always	Sometimes	Never	
✓			Think about and plan what you will write?
		✓	Think about what your reader will need to understand what you've written? What kinds of vocabulary words will you use? What important ideas and details must be included?
	✓		Decide what type of language and grammar you will use? Will your writing be formal or informal? Who will read your piece?
	✓		Decide what structure you will use in your writing? Paragraphs? Diagrams? Complete sentences? A form of poetry?
	✓		Sketch out your overall plan in a visual way? Do you use a graphic organizer or an outline?

While writing something, do you...

Always	Sometimes	Never	
	✓		Write a rough draft just to get your ideas down first?
✓			Read and reread parts you've written?
	✓		Freely revise and move things around to try things out?
	✓		Ask yourself, How can I make this clearer or better organized? Would a title or headings help?
	✓		Add or delete information as needed? Evaluate your writing?
	✓		Talk with someone about your writing to get feedback or ideas? (This cannot be done during the State ELA test, though.)

After writing something, do you...

Always	Sometimes	Never	
_____	✓	_____	Read and reread the whole thing as if you were the reader? Listen to what you've written as if you're hearing it for the first time? Listen critically to see what you need to change, add, or cut out completely?
_____	_____	✓	Read your piece through one more time JUST to edit for grammar and spelling?
_____	✓	_____	Share your writing with someone to get feedback? (Of course, you cannot use this strategy during the State test!)

WRITING PRACTICE

Now that you've thought about your writing and you've read the sample passage about Axel City, it's time to create your own imaginary city. Write an essay about an imaginary city based on a theme of your choice. Where would you like to live? In a football city? In an animal town? You decide. In your essay, describe how the city would be designed and how people would make a living there. Use the writing strategies described. Possible responses are given at the end of this section.

My writing process before writing:

1. What is your plan?

   Math city

2. What do you think your reader will need to understand what you write? What kinds of vocabulary words will you use?

   what the city looks like. Beautiful.

   Expensive. Affordable.

3. What important ideas and details do you want to be sure to include?

The different names that are dor
buildings.

4. What type of language and grammar will you use? (Formal or informal? Who will read your piece?)

Informal, Aleks, daddy, mommy.

5. What structure will you use in your writing? Paragraphs? Diagrams? Complete sentences? A form of poetry?

Paragraphs.

6. Sketch your overall plan in a visual way. Examples: a graphic organizer or an outline.

Sketch here:

Now, it's time to write your essay. Practice each of these strategies. Check them off as you use them. You might use some strategies several times.

Strategies while writing:

___✓___ Write a rough draft just to get your ideas down first.

_____ Read and reread parts you've written.

_____ Freely revise and move sentences around to try things out.

_____ Ask yourself, How can I make this clearer or better organized? Would a title or headings help?

_____ Add or delete information as needed? Evaluate your writing.

_____ Talk with someone about your writing to get feed-back or ideas.

Math city is a wonderful city, all based on math.
Our police department, D.D.D. or Division Department
Division, is one of the best but we barely have
any crime. Our precise and 100% accuret Math
Money bank is a wonderful bank with 1% intrest
loans (gaining annually) and is run by Mr. Multiplication.
The very same man who is the soul Caretaker
and founder of Multiplication Mapping. A very

popular car company Worldwide! He also owns subtraction subway, Calculator clothes and, Sqare Root screams which is an amusment park which he runs with the mayor Mrs. factor. Mrs. Factor has been mayor for 2 years now And has been keeping the city comfortable and running. The biggest company is run by her brother Mr. Book. He owns the business workplace. It is a company where 95% of Math citys population works. The economy is nice with many sightseeing places that are 100% natural and have not been touched by anything except Tiki Torches. There is a huge lakec and many parks with swimming area's. About 9000 people live here. All of them love Math city and we hope more people will join the fun!

Finally, check your after-writing strategies to really polish your essay. Have you…

_____ Read and reread the whole thing as if you were the reader? Listened to what you wrote as if you were hearing it for the first time? Listened critically to see what you need to change, add, or cut out completely?

_____ Read through your piece one more time JUST to edit for grammar and spelling?

_____ Shared your writing with someone to get feedback?

POSSIBLE RESPONSES

My writing process before writing:

1. What is your plan?

I'm planning to write about a town where animals are treated with respect and are not used for food or products or as service animals.

2. What do you think your reader will need to understand what you write? What kinds of vocabulary words will you use?

I'll need to be sensitive to my audience and not say grotesque things about animal abuse. I'll use vocabulary a sixth-grader could understand because I want people at that grade level to think about animal rights.

3. What important ideas and details do you want to be sure to include?

People will be the residents in this town. It won't be a town run by animals. The people will just be sensitive to animals' rights. They won't try to change the world, but their town will be a place where they don't take advantage of animals.

4. What type of language and grammar will you use? (Formal or informal? Who will read this piece?)

This piece will be read by sixth-graders. It will be written like a formal report, though, so that they take my ideas seriously.

5. What structure will you use in your writing? Paragraphs? Diagrams? Complete sentences? A form of poetry?

I'll have a title, an introductory paragraph, a section about the structure of the town, a section about the economy, and a conclusion.

6. Sketch your overall plan in a visual way. Examples: a graphic organizer or an outline.

Animal Town, USA

   I. Introduction
      A. who will live in the town
      B. how animals will be treated
      C. why animals will be treated this way
  II. The structure of the town
      A. laws protecting animals as well as people
      B. the safety of animals and humans
      C. the responsibilities of animals and humans
      D. living arrangements
  III. The economy of the town
      A. jobs
      B. tourism
  IV. Conclusion
      A. restatement of purpose
      B. a better world

SAMPLE ESSAY

Animal Town, USA

Kelly Lassonde

Animal Town, USA, is a little town far away where people and animals happily live together. The only people allowed to live in the town are vegetarians. Any animal is allowed to live in Animal Town, but most of the animals there are sick or orphaned. It is the humans' job to make them feel better and to raise them so they can live on their own. The animals of Animal Town are very special to the people there. It is the people's job to take good care of the animals.

There are not many laws in Animal Town. Usually everything is very quiet and peaceful. The few laws they do have treat all humans and animals equally. No one in the town can eat meat. There are only eight-hour workdays so no one will be overworked. Also, every sick or orphaned animal that comes into the town must be given a home. Everyone must clean up after themselves so the town will stay clean. All human families live with a group of four or five animals. The animals live in a separate house, but right next to the humans' homes.

Animal Town is a farming town. Every member of the town works to grow and harvest food. The humans do all of the work such as planting seeds and making tools. Very few people are allowed to come into Animal Town during the week, but on weekends there is a carnival. People from all over come to the carnival to buy the food the town grows. There are always rides at this carnival. The animals love to play with the children who come.

Animal Town is a very peaceful place where animals and humans live together on equal ground. It is surrounded by fields and hills. Many people come to have fun because it is so peaceful and happy. For the people and animals it is a better world.

LISTENING STRATEGIES

What happens when you listen to someone? Does your mind start to wander? Do you start to think about what you're going to do when you get home? Do you think about the speaker's jewelry or hair while you're listening and then lose track of what is being said? It happens. The question is, how do you stop yourself from getting distracted? You have to practice ACTIVE LISTENING.

With active listening, you focus on the message and on what is being said. You push everything else out of your mind and concentrate on the story or events. Practice the following strategies good listeners use the next time you are listening to your teacher or someone else read to you. Or borrow some books on tape or books on CDs from your local library. Practice actively listening to the stories. If you find it difficult to apply the strategies for a long time, gradually increase the amount of time you focus. Start with just a few minutes. Each day add 15 seconds to the length of time you focus. You'll be surprised how quickly you can build up your listening skills. Here are some strategies:

■ Avoid physical distractions. Close your eyes and visualize the story as you are listening. Where are the characters? What do they look like? What are they doing? BUT DON'T FALL ASLEEP! Or try looking right at the reader's face or mouth. The point is to avoid looking around and letting your mind wander.

- Put yourself inside the story. Think of yourself as one of the characters or think about how the characters get along with each other. Or think about the sequence of events.

- Do not get hung up on one or two vocabulary words that you don't understand.

- Should you lose track of what is happening, just pick up the story from where the reader is right then. It is better to listen to and understand part of the story than to become worried and just give up. You'll be surprised how you can pick up the story even after a lapse in understanding or listening actively.

- Imagine your ears have grown twice their size and are absorbing the story, all of the main ideas, and the supporting details.

TEST-TAKING STRATEGIES

Tests and assessments are a way of life. School isn't the only place where you'll have to take tests, so you might as well get used to them. As a citizen you'll probably take a test to get your driver's permit. Many colleges require tests before they accept you. Employers often give tests before they hire you. Tests are unavoidable. Throughout this book you will learn specific strategies for taking the New York State Grade 6 ELA test. You will get lots of practice to help you feel confident in what you are doing.

The best advice for test taking, though, is to go to the test prepared. The better prepared you are, the more relaxed and confident you will be. Be well rested and ready to meet the challenge. Think of the test as a way to show off what you know and what you can do.

ONLINE RESOURCES

For ABC's of the Writing Process go to: *www.angelfire. com/wi/writingprocess/*

Want to learn more about the writing process? This site describes the steps, gives examples, and also lists several links that you can go to for more information.

Test-taking Strategies, Skills, and Techniques *http://www.testtakingtips.com/test/index.htm* and Tips for Better Test Taking *http://www.studygs.net/tsttak1.htm*

Want to know how to study for multiple-choice, essay, and true-false tests? These two web sites give all kinds of tips on preparing for all kinds of tests.

What Good Readers Do From A to Z *http://www. campusschool.dsu.edu/teacherslounge/CA%20ABC.ppt#12*

This web site gives tips on reading for each letter of the alphabet! It will give you some ideas about how to improve yourself as a reader, such as reading lots of books and having a purpose for reading.

CONGRATULATIONS!

Now you know what literacy means. You have learned about and practiced effective strategies that good readers, writers, and listeners use. Sharpening your literacy skills will benefit you not just in testing situations but in life in general.

Next, you should continue on to Chapter 2. There, you will get an overview of the New York State Grade 6 ELA test. You will learn about the New York State Learning Standards, too.

OVERVIEW OF THE NEW YORK STATE GRADE 6 ELA TEST

Now that you have obtained some ideas about reading, writing, and listening effectively from Chapter 1, you are ready to start asking questions about the test. This chapter gives answers to some of the most frequently asked questions about the sixth-grade test. The details explained in this chapter will give you an idea of what to expect.

WHY DO I TAKE THESE TESTS?

This is a valid question that you have a right to ask. Why do schools in New York State require you to take a State test in English Language Arts every year from Grades 3 through 8? Why must we take time for these tests, especially if they do not count as a grade? There are two ways to answer this question. One way is simple, and the other is complicated. Both answers are important to understand.

The simple answer is that these tests help your teachers, your family, and you think about how your school can do its best to teach you. If you do well on the tests, we—your teachers, family, and you—can assume your schooling is on track and should continue down the same successful path. But if you do not do well on the tests or certain parts of the tests, it means we have to look more closely at what we are doing. Your teachers will look for a way to teach so you and your peers will be more successful. You and your family will think about what you can do to improve your learning. In short, you take these tests so we can figure out how to help you become a well-developed literate person in today's world.

Now, here is the more complicated answer to your question. Teachers in New York State do not haphazardly decide what to teach every day. They have long-term goals they work toward to help you develop as learners from year to year. They plan their daily classroom lessons based on a set of skills and knowledge called the New York State Learning Standards. These Learning Standards are published by the New York State Department of Education. There are Standards in

- English Language Art,
- Mathematics, Science, and Technology,
- Social Studies,
- the Arts, and other areas.

These Standards are the core of what all students should know and be able to do by the time they leave high school.

There are four English Language Arts Learning Standards:

1. Students will read, write, listen, and speak for information and understanding;
2. Students will read, write, listen, and speak for literary response and expression;
3. Students will read, write, listen, and speak for critical analysis and evaluation; and
4. Students will read, write, listen, and speak for social interaction.

Figure 2.1 shows some examples of what the four Learning Standards include in the sixth grade.

Standard 1: Language for Information and Understanding

Can you

- use library resources to write reports,
- compare and contrast ideas, and
- take notes to organize ideas?

Standard 2: Language for Literary Response and Expression

Can you

- tell the difference between the characteristics of different types of texts, such as fables, fantasy, and biography;
- identify the setting, plot, and characters in a text; and
- write interpretive essays about texts?

Standard 3: Language for Critical Analysis and Evaluation

Can you

- express opinions and make judgments,
- evaluate the accuracy of information, and
- recognize how one's point of view can influence his or her opinion?

Standard 4: Language for Social Interaction

Can you

- recognize the type of language that is appropriate in various situations,
- share meaningful reading experiences with your peers, and
- develop a personal voice in your writing?

Figure 2.1   Examples of Grade 6 English Language Arts Learning Standards

How do teachers, families, and students themselves find out how they are doing with the Learning Standards? You will want to know as a student what kind of progress you are making as you move through the grades. Do you, for example, understand how to read a book and learn information from it at the same level as other sixth-grade students in the state? In New York State, the ELA tests students take in Grades 3 through 8 are standardized. This means that every student taking a test works under similar conditions. For example, they answer the same questions, they have the same amount of time to do the test, they are given the same directions, and the tests are scored the same way. The questions on the tests are based on the first three ELA Learning Standards. Standard 4 is not assessed. Figure 2.2 shows the approximate percentage of questions on Grade 6 ELA test that are based on Standards 1, 2, and 3. This brings us right back to where we started when we said teachers base their daily lessons around the standards. When everything is on track,

teachers' lessons are based on the Standards,

↓

you learn from the lessons,

↓

you take tests that are also based on the Standards,

↓

and your test answers show you are reaching the goals of the Standards!

Standard	Percentage
1	36
2	44.5
3	19.5

Figure 2.2   Percentage of Questions That Test Each Standard

The complicated answer to your question, Why do we have these tests?, then is that your teachers, your family, and you want to be sure that daily classroom lessons and your yearly progress are both on the right path. That is, they are on the path that allows every student to reach the goals of the New York State Learning Standards. It is all about you and what you need to be successful. Therefore, it is for your own benefit that you do your best on these tests.

WHAT IS THE TEST LIKE?

The rest of this chapter will help you become more familiar with the testing process. Knowing what to expect ahead of time will help you feel more comfortable when you actually sit down to take a test. We will share with you information about

- when and how the test will be given,
- what the school's responsibilities are,
- what your responsibilities are,
- the parts of the test, and
- how the test will be scored.

As you read this chapter, highlight the parts that you think are most important to remember. With a pencil, jot in the margins any questions that come to mind as you are reading. Ask your teacher or a family member to help you answer these questions before you take the test.

WHEN DO I TAKE THE TEST?

The sixth-grade ELA test is given in the middle of January each year. It is made up of three parts. Each part is called a book. You will take one book per day for three days in a row. Each part is timed. You will have about one hour to finish each book. Figure 2.3 gives more information about the test schedule and the types of questions on the test. For a short-response question you will be asked to write a short answer. You might complete a graphic organizer or write a three- to five-sentence response to a question. For an extended-response question you will be asked to write a longer, more complete answer. These responses should be a page or two long, like an essay.

Day	Book	Selection	Test Time (minutes)	Prep Time (minutes)
1	1	Reading 26 multiple-choice questions	55	10
2	2	Listening and Writing 3 short-response questions and 1 extended-response question	45	15
3	3	Reading and Writing 3 short-response questions and 1 extended-response question	60	10

Figure 2.3 Test Scheduling Information

WHAT MATERIALS DO I NEED TO BRING?

Bring three no. 2 pencils with erasers. Sharpen all three pencils before the test. Your teacher will provide all the other testing materials, such as test books and answer sheets.

WHAT ARE THE SCHOOL ADMINISTRATOR'S RESPONSIBILITIES?

It is the responsibility of the school administrator or principal to be sure

- he or she has the right amount of test materials for each classroom;
- tests are kept in a secure, safe place;
- other arrangements for testing are made ahead of time in case stormy weather causes a school closing;
- students with Individualized Education Plans (IEPs) or 504 Plans are given their accommodations, which means that the way the test is given may be changed in a way that will help students with disabilities;
- teachers and assistants have been well trained to give the test and provide for accommodations; and
- the test is scored fairly and all scores are reported to the New York State Education Department.

WHAT ARE THE TEACHER'S RESPONSIBILITIES?

It is the responsibility of the teacher to be sure

- the classroom is organized in a way that students will be able to do their best;
- all the testing materials are ready;
- students are prepared for the test each day;
- he or she understands what accommodations are allowed for all students; see Figures 2.4 and 2.5, which show what accommodations are allowed on the ELA test;
- he or she is familiar with the directions, the passages (especially the one read aloud to the students), and how to use the manual;
- he or she reads the directions clearly and at an appropriate speed;
- he or she monitors the test; and
- he or she knows how to manage the time limits on the test.

BOOK 1

What may be read aloud to ALL students?

The bold-faced test directions that come before each passage or test question number. No other parts of this section may be read aloud to the students.

BOOK 2

What may be read aloud to ALL students?

The bold-faced test directions that come before each passage or test question number.

What may be read if students' Individualized Educational Plans (IEPs) or 504 Plans state "tests read"?

The bold-faced test directions and all the questions. Also, they may be read aloud more times than stated in the teacher's directions if accommodations include this.

BOOK 3

What may be read aloud to ALL students?

The bold-faced test directions that come before each passage or test question number. No other parts of this section may be read aloud to the students.

WHEN WRITING

What may NOT be used by ANY students?

Spell checkers and grammar checkers.

What may be used if students' Individualized Educational Plans or 504 Plans allow for them?

Scribes, tape recorders, or word processors (without spell checkers or grammar checkers).

Figure 2.4 Accommodation Questions

- Extra time
- A separate place
- A third reading of the listening section
- Direct translations (a bilingual dictionary or glossary)

Figure 2.5 Possible Accommodations for Students Who Are Limited-English Proficient (LEP)

WHAT ARE THE STUDENT'S RESPONSIBILITIES?

It is the responsibility of the student to be sure he or she

- is ready for the test;
- listens closely to the directions;
- reads the passages carefully and closely;
- listens closely to the passages that are read to him or her;
- gives thoughtful responses;
- carefully manages time during the test; and
- does his or her very best.

WHAT ARE THE THREE BOOKS OF THE TEST?

The three books are Book 1: Reading, Book 2: Listening and Writing, and Book 3: Reading and Writing. They test ELA Standards 1 through 3. Each book is described fully in this book in Chapters 3 through 5. You will practice how to answer sample questions. But first, here is a quick introduction to each book.

Book 1: Reading has four or five passages for you to read on your own. Each passage is followed by a few multiple-choice questions about the passage. Your answers will show how well you understand the passages. Can you get information from, interpret, respond to, or critically analyze the passages? These passages may be fiction or nonfiction, poems or stories, or a variety of other types of reading. See Appendix A for a listing of literary genres. The vocabulary and content are both relevant to what you have been reading in class and for homework. Remember, Book 1 tests Standards 1 through 3. You will fill in circles on an answer sheet that is separate from your test book.

In Book 2: Listening and Writing, one passage will be read to you. You will hear it read twice. Then you will be asked to answer two questions with short answers and another question with a longer answer. Your answers will show how well you understand and can express your understanding of the readings in writing. The passage may be a short story, a poem, or another type of literary writing. You will not get to see the questions before the passage is read to you, but you will be able to take lots of notes while you are listening. The passage you hear will be similar to passages you have been read during class time. Book 2 tests Standard 2. You will write your responses right in the test book.

Book 3: Reading and Writing has two paired passages. This means that you will read one passage, write short answers to questions on it, read another passage, write short answers to questions on it, and then read a third passage and write a more complete answer to a question about both passages. Book 3 tests Standard 3. You will write your responses right in the test book.

HOW IS THE TEST SCORED?

Your answers on the ELA test will show

- if you understand what the passages mean,
- if you can use information from the passages to support ideas,

- if you can organize your ideas,
- if you can use language effectively and expressively,
- if you can spell and punctuate correctly, and
- if you can use paragraphing and grammar correctly.

The scoring is shown graphically in Figure 2.6. In Book 1, each of the 26 multiple-choice answers is worth 1 point. The questions in Books 2 and 3 are scored together as a cluster. The 4 questions in Book 2 are worth a total of 5 points. The 4 questions in Book 3 are worth a total of 5 points. Finally, question 30 in Book 2 and question 34 in Book 3 are used to check your writing skills. Using a rubric, your answers to these two questions can earn up to 3 additional points. See Appendix C: Sample Scoring Rubrics to learn more about how the short and extended writing responses and writing mechanics are scored. Use these rubrics to check your progress.

Books	What Each Book Tests	Questions	Type of Question	Maximum Points
1	Reading	1–26	Multiple choice	26
2	Listening and writing	27–30	Short and long (extended) written responses	5
3	Reading and writing	31–34	Short and long (extended) written responses	5
2 and 3	Writing mechanics	30 and 34	Long (extended) responses for questions 30 and 34 are used to score writing mechanics (These are not additional test questions.)	3

Figure 2.6 Point Distribution of Questions

WHAT ELSE SHOULD I KNOW ABOUT THE TEST?

In Chapters 3, 4, and 5, you will use what you have learned so far to practice answering sample test questions. You will learn strategies and skills about reading, writing, and listening that will not only help you do well on the test but will also help you develop as a literate person.

ONLINE RESOURCES

You will find these web sites helpful to learn more about the setup of the Grade 6 ELA test and the ideas behind the State Learning Standards.

■ To see a set of all the New York State Learning Standards, go to the State Education Department's website at *http://usny.nysed.gov/teachers/nyslearning standards.html.*

■ To see the complete set of English Language Arts Learning Standards, go to *http://www.emsc.nysed.gov/ ciai/ela/elacore.doc.*

■ To see more practice ELA tests, go to *http://www. nysedregents.org/testing/elaei/06exams/home.htm.*

CONGRATULATIONS!

Now you have a lot of information about the test. You know there are three books and what each book focuses on. Knowing all this in advance will help you feel more relaxed and confident on the test days. You aren't going into the test in complete darkness. Instead, you have a pretty bright flashlight to lead you along.

Next, continue on to Chapter 3, which is all about Book 1, the reading part of the test. You'll learn all about how to complete multiple-choice questions as you practice with interesting reading passages.

BOOK 1: READING

DESCRIPTION

What is Book 1 about? Book 1 is the reading section of the State test. In this section, you will be given several different passages to read. You may be asked to read a short story, a folk tale, a poem, or an example of some other literary genre. You may also be asked to read an item from an informational or nonfiction genre, such as a newspaper article, an essay, or a short biography or autobiography. (See Appendix A for a list of literary genres.) You will apply the reading skills you have learned in class and in this book by answering reading comprehension questions based on Standards 1 through 3. Your answers will show what you understand about the passages.

Book 1 contains four or five reading passages. After reading each passage, you will carefully read and answer between 4 and 7 multiple-choice questions. There are 26 multiple-choice questions all together. Each answer is worth 1 point. You will have 55 minutes to read all the passages and answer all the questions. Your teacher will go over the directions with you the day of the test so you will know how to mark your answers. But a preview follows so you will know what to expect.

TEST DIRECTIONS

Your teacher will pass out a booklet that includes the passages and questions and a separate answer sheet. You may make notes in your test booklet. As you read, you may want to underline or highlight phrases or important information, or you might jot notes to yourself in the margins. You may write notes in the question booklet to help you understand your reading better. But your answers must be marked on the answer sheet to get credit for them.

When you mark your answers on the answer sheet, be sure to

- check that you match the number of the question in the booklet to the number on the answer sheet;
- use a no. 2 pencil to fill in the circle for the letter matching your answer;
- make a heavy, black mark;
- erase completely and remark your answer sheet if you decide to change any of your answers; and
- avoid making any stray marks on the answer sheet that might be confused with an answer.

In the practice tests in Chapters 6 and 7 of this book, sample answer sheets are provided for you to use with those tests. You will be able to practice the tips you have just read.

Book 1 measures how well you understand what you read. Be sure to answer the questions based on the passage, not on your personal experiences or opinion. You may look back at the passages and your notes as much as you want. You must work alone, though.

TESTING ACCOMMODATIONS

If you are a student with a disability or you have an individualized education program (IEP), you may be eligible for testing accommodations. For Book 1, because it measures how well you understand what you read, only the directions—no other parts of the book—may be read aloud to you. Your teacher will be sure you are given any accommodations you are allowed.

BREAKDOWN OF QUESTIONS

Remember, the State test is based on ELA Learning Standards 1, 2, and 3. In Book 1, here is how the questions break down:

Standard	Percentage of Questions
1: Language for Information and Understanding	36%
2: Language for Literary Response and Expression	44.5%
3: Language for Critical Analysis and Evaluation	19.5%

Knowing this breakdown will help you be prepared for the types of questions you will see in Book 1. For example, you know there will be more questions about Standard 2 than any other Standard.

GETTING STARTED

Next, you will learn strategies for answering questions based on Standards 1 through 3. Keep in mind that all of these strategies and skills will pay off by improving your reading comprehension.

As you work, read the description of each strategy, and then think

What do I usually do when I come to something like this in my reading?

Start with what you know and what already works for you. Then read our suggestions to add to your strategy. Here we go!

STRATEGIES FOR COMPLETING MULTIPLE-CHOICE QUESTIONS

The good news about multiple-choice questions is that the correct answer is there—somewhere. You just have to find it! Here are some strategies some students find helpful in tackling multiple-choice questions.

1. Take one minute to skim through the passage and questions quickly before carefully reading the passage. Underline one or two key words in each question that you will look for as you read the passage.

2. In your first time reading through, you want to concentrate on understanding what the passage is about overall. Try to get into the story and hear the message the author is trying to get across to you. Read the passage carefully. Apply the reading strategies you learned in Chapter 1 as you read. Also, keep the questions in the back of your head. If you happen to find some of the answers while you are reading, put a little checkmark in the margin so you can come back to that spot when you are answering the questions. Do not stop to answer questions in the middle of reading, though.

3. Answer the questions you can answer easily first. Circle the correct choices in your test booklet.

4. Go back to the passage to reread parts to help you answer questions you are not sure of. Circle the correct choices in your test booklet.

5. Before moving on to the next passage, transfer your answers to the answer sheet. By doing this, you will be sure to put the answers in the right places on the answer sheet, especially if you skipped some hard questions the first time through.

STUCK ON A MULTIPLE-CHOICE QUESTION? MORE STRATEGIES

If you really cannot figure out an answer, try one of these strategies:

1. Process of elimination. Cross off the choices that you know are wrong. Then reread the parts of the passage that will help you eliminate all but one choice.
2. True or false. If you are better at true/false questions, try reading each choice as a true/false statement. Read the stem (the first part of the question) and the first choice as a statement. Is it true or false? If it is true, you have found the right answer! (This strategy works only with questions where the choice completes the stem sentence.)
3. Cover the answers. Cover everything but the stem (the first part) of the question. Try to guess the answer first. Then, read the choices and decide which comes closest.
4. Take your best guess. This is your final strategy. Do not leave any answer blank. If you cannot figure out an answer, do not linger too long. Remember, this is a timed test. Make an intelligent guess and put a star by the question in your booklet. If you have time left after you have finished everything else, go back to this question.

STUDENT CHECKLIST OF STRATEGIES TO USE

Use this checklist, which summarizes the strategies described in the following sections, as you work through the sample questions. After each question, write down which strategies helped you.

CHECKLIST OF STRATEGIES

Multiple-choice strategies:

_____ Skim questions before reading passage.

_____ Read passage carefully and completely.

_____ Answer questions you can first.

_____ Reread parts of the passage and answer other questions.

Collecting information strategies:

_____ Consider clues in the text structure.

_____ Look back. Reread.

_____ Identify facts and opinions.

_____ Look for context clues.

Responding to literature strategies:

_____ Interpret the text.

_____ Monitor your comprehension as you read.

_____ Get to know the characters well.

_____ Look for clues in the words.

_____ Use what you know about the reading genre.

Main idea strategies:

_____ Use title as a clue.

_____ Check the first and final paragraphs for clues.

_____ Question the writer's main message.

_____ Compare choices against each other.

_____ Circle supporting details and connect ideas.

_____ Visualize the paragraph.

SAMPLE QUESTIONS WITH GUIDED PRACTICE

As you work through the guided practices in this chapter, check the "From the Sideline" features to monitor your thinking. Use the strategies in these features as guides to help you do your best. Check off each item as you monitor it.

STANDARD 1: LANGUAGE FOR INFORMATION AND UNDERSTANDING

The questions in Book 1 may test these reading skills:

- Identifying organizational formats—How is the information in an article organized? Is a problem presented and then a solution given? Are events sequenced or in time order? Is there a cause and then an effect given? Are two items compared or contrasted?

- Collecting and interpreting information—You are asked to remember something specifically from the passage or you may be asked to take the information you are given and draw conclusions to interpret what it means.

- Distinguishing fact from opinion—What information is true and what is based on what someone feels or thinks?

- Identifying what is implied—You may be asked to identify information that is not directly stated in the passage but is implied.

- Using context clues—Unfamiliar words may be used. How can you figure out what they mean based on what you know about the rest of the sentence or passage?

Strategies for Collecting Information From Your Reading

Texts are wonderful sources of information. But we need to know how to organize, sort, and categorize the information we get from texts to really understand it. To effectively gain information from what you read, try these strategies:

1. Text structure. Examine how the text is organized. Knowing this will help you categorize the information in your head so you can connect what you already know to this new information. Is the text organized in one of these ways?

   a. Problem followed by solution

   Example: A character is having a difficult time with math in school (problem), and then he gets a math tutor who helps him understand math, providing an answer (solution) that solves or eliminates the problem.

   b. Sequenced or in time order

   Example: The author tells us what he does from the time he wakes up until the time he goes to sleep at night.

   c. Cause and effect

   Example: A character sleeps late, so she is late for school. This causes a series of unfortunate events to occur. She has to rush through a test that has already started and ends up failing it. Then, because she failed the test, she is told by her parents that she can't go to the school dance, and so on. The unfortunate events are the result of sleeping late.

   d. Compare and contrast

   Example: A story tells about the similarities and differences of two diverse cultures, such as the Navaho and the Apache.

   e. Hyperlinks

   Example: Clicking on the name "Henry Ford" on a web page about cars brings you to a story about him.

2. Look back. You will not be able to remember everything you read, but try to remember where important
information is located. Make notes in the margin to
highlight essential details.

3. Fact versus opinion. Classify which information is
factual and which is based on someone's personal
opinions. Sometimes this is less obvious than at other
times. A fact can be proven. An opinion is questionable or arguable.

4. Use context clues. If your teacher has asked you to
write down vocabulary words from sentences, you
have already experienced using context clues. In a sentence or passage, the context refers to the words and
paragraphs around a word or phrase. If you come
across an unfamiliar word or phrase, you can sometimes use the overall meaning of the sentence to figure
out what the word means. Sometimes authors give
clues to a word's meaning by

   a. giving examples in words, pictures, or diagrams;
   b. using synonyms or antonyms; and
   c. using signal terms such as *for example, like,
      unlike,* and *such as.*

From the sideline: Tips for Completing the Passage
- *Read all the directions carefully.*
- *Think about the answer before choosing your response.*

Standard 1, Sample Passage A

Directions: **Read this passage about the Niagara
Aerospace Museum. Then answer questions 1 through 3.**

---

legacy—anything that has been handed down from one
generation to the next

innovation—an invention or a creative idea

NIAGARA AEROSPACE MUSEUM

Home | History | Tours | Kids' Zone | Educators | Digital Library | Membership | About Us | Contacts

http://aerospace.bfn.org/index.htm

Credit: Niagara Aerospace Museum

The "Right Stuff" Started Right Here!

Western New York is the home of an incredible number of aviation achievements in the Twentieth Century. This area of the country has attracted adventurers and scientists who created a legacy of standing aircraft and aerospace accomplishments. Although many of the companies have moved away or disappeared, some of them remain in this area. Many of the innovations still contribute to the aviation and space industries today.

This is a 1918 Curtiss JN4H "Jenny."   © Fred Sgrosso

Western New York was one of the first major centers of America's aviation development from the early 1900s. It was an industry leader that made many significant contributions to aerospace as well.

The world's largest aircraft manufacturing plant in Buffalo, New York, produced Curtiss flying boats and "Jenny" trainer planes during World War I. Curtiss also produced the US Navy's racing hydroplanes that established speed records in the Pulitzer, Schneider Cup, and other popular races.

The purpose of the museum is to preserve the memory and spirit of Western New York aviation workers and pioneers by presenting their stories and safekeeping the artifacts of their heritage. The museum seeks to keep their memory and spirit alive by demonstrating and displaying those artifacts in a manner that will both make future generations proud and capture and spur their interests to continue the Western New York aerospace tradition. Our museum is in the process of adding a Kids' Zone. Here families will stop and enjoy a little fun together. The museum's purpose is to honor and educate people about our proud local history and the remarkable and innovative people who have contributed to the many breakthroughs here.

Museum Background

> **Defunct**—inactive

The Niagara Aerospace Museum first opened its doors in 1998 in a defunct department store located in a Niagara Falls, New York, mall. Generous private donors funded the project. In 2002, the museum made a much-needed move downtown to the Ira G. Ross Center located at Third and Niagara Streets. Here the museum was able to greatly expand its collection and exhibit more of the many donations it had acquired, including those made by local technicians and inventors. The additional space has allowed for the display of several aircraft including a Bell P-39 "Airacobra," a reproduction of an early World War I-era Curtiss "Pusher," and a replica of the world-famous rocket-belt (of James Bond and Super Bowl fame), all of which have Western New York roots.

Check out our "Tours" and "Kids' Zone" line above for on-site opportunities!

1. This information was most likely found

    A. on the World Wide Web.

    B. in an encyclopedia.

    C. in a textbook.

    D. in a magazine advertisement.

    *Strategies you used:*_____

2. Which of the following is an opinion?

    A. Western New York was one of the first major centers of America's aviation development from the early 1900s.

    B. The museum's purpose is to honor and educate people about our proud local history and the remarkable and innovative people who have contributed to the many breakthroughs here.

    C. Here families will stop and enjoy a little fun together.

    D. Western New York is the home of an incredible number of aviation achievements in the Twentieth Century.

    *Strategies you used:*_____

3. The use of the word *aerospace* in the name of the museum tells us we will most likely find what types of artifacts at the museum?

    A. helicopters

    B. astronauts and space rockets

    C. all types of vehicles that travel through the earth's space and atmosphere

    D. science fiction aircraft

    *Strategies you used:*_____

Answers for Sample Passage A

1. By paying close attention to detail, you will notice that this information has the look of a web page from the World Wide Web. There are links along the top and the bottom that will lead you to connected web pages about the museum's digital library, tours, membership, and so on. Also, the web address for the site appears along the top. Finally, the last line of text refers to links, which seals the deal that this is a web site. The correct answer is A. Choices B, C, and D would not have link buttons.

2. For this question, you have to know the difference between a fact and an opinion. Choices A and D are true things about the history of Western New York. Choice B describes what the museum sees as its purpose, so that it is also true. Choice C is the opinion. In the author's opinion the Kids' Zone will entertain families. This cannot be considered true for all families unless all have tried it, though!

3. From the text and the picture on the web page you learn that the museum contains all kinds of aircraft, both real and fictional, that travel through space. You use context clues. Choices A, B, and D list examples of the vehicles you would find there, but choice C includes all of the kinds of vehicles described in the other choices. So, the answer is C.

> *From the sideline: Tips for Completing the Passage*
> ▪ *Read all the directions carefully.*
> ▪ *Think about the answer before choosing your response.*

Standard 1, Sample Passage B

Directions: **Read the following excerpt of a news article about global warming and its probable effects on animals. Then answer questions 1 through 3.**

DISAPPEARING ICE

Alison Black

The coldest and most remote places in the world are the North and South Poles. They may have a lot of animal visitors but few humans venture there. If you have ever thought of going, now is the time. Why? Both of the poles have started to change drastically due to global warming. Ice and snow in these regions are melting so quickly they are setting records.

This disappearing ice may impact life on earth in many ways. The rising sea levels around the world are placing both animals and people at risk. Many animals such as the polar bear and seal depend upon ice for survival. Oceans are becoming diluted and less salty as water from melted ice makes its way into our rivers and oceans. In addition, the waters are warming, placing creatures that live in or near the ice at risk.

Because the impact of climate change upon the North and South Pole regions is becoming more and more evident, we are being asked by experts to think about the way we live. Carbon dioxide and other greenhouse gases responsible for trapping excess heat in our atmosphere are created by the fossil fuels used in our cars, power plants, and factories. However, we may be able to save the disappearing ice if we produce fewer of these gases. If we can save this disappearing ice, we will also help to protect ourselves, our oceans, and other living creatures on this earth.

We all need to consider some Pole-friendly activities such as bicycling, walking, and using public transportation. Even simple actions at home such as switching to efficient compact fluorescent light bulbs and turning off the lights in rooms when we're not using them will help. Finally, asking that our politicians fight for the environment can also help.

"Small things would make a difference," Dr. Steve Rintoul, a noted oceanographer, says, "if everyone did them."

1. According to this article, experts are encouraging people to be Pole-friendly

   A. because fossil fuels are becoming extinct.

   B. to stop the climate change.

   C. because it is the law.

   D. to save money.

   *Strategies you used:*_____

2. Read this sentence from the article.

   "Small things would make a difference," Dr. Steve Rintoul, a noted oceanographer, says, "if everyone did them."

   The author ends with this statement

   A. to shock the reader.

   B. to make the article more believable.

   C. to discourage the reader.

   D. to challenge the reader.

   *Strategies you used:*_____

3. Why does the article imply that biking is a Pole-friendly activity?

   A. It helps people stay in shape.

   B. It is less expensive than driving a car.

   C. It can help to protect the polar ice.

   D. It can be done at the North and South Poles.

   *Strategies you used:*_____

Answers for Sample Passage B

1. The correct answer is B because the other choices are not even mentioned in the article. While some of the other choices may be true, the key phrase is "According to this article."

2. The correct answer is D. While this article tends to be very serious and overwhelming for the reader, the author ends with a thread of hope that if we all pitch in we can beat global warming. The rest of the article shocks the reader, not this final statement. The statement does not make the article more believable because it does not present more supporting information. The statement does not discourage the reader but rather leads the reader to think there is hope.

3. Biking, walking, and taking public transportation may help people stay in shape, be less expensive than driving a car, and can even be done at the North and South Poles. But, the reason this article implies in the sentences just before the one about biking, walking, and public transportation is that they can help save the polar ice, the oceans, and us. Fewer gases are produced by these means of transportation than by driving cars. Therefore, less heat is trapped in our atmosphere. The correct answer is C.

STANDARD 2: LANGUAGE FOR LITERARY RESPONSE AND EXPRESSION

The questions in Book 1 may test your skills in

■ Interpreting texts—Can you tell what the author is trying to reveal by a particular part of the passage or by something a character says or does?

■ Using literary elements—Can you identify the **setting**, **plot**, and characters of a passage? How does the author use these **elements** in the passage to interest readers? What is the **conflict** in the story?

- Noticing character development—Can you identify the ways a character changes from the beginning to the end of a story or what the character's motivation is?

- Understanding literary devices—How does the author use imagery, similes, metaphors, or personification to create meaning?

- Recognizing signal words—Can you identify words that signal organization in a passage? Some of these words might indicate that a story takes place over time, such as *finally, in addition, in the end, earlier, later,* and *next.*

- Identifying characteristics of different genres—Do you know the features of various genres, such as realistic fiction, autobiography, tall tale, and so on? (See Appendix A for a list of various literary genres.)

Strategies for Responding to Literature

When you are trying to understand and respond to a passage, think of yourself as a detective who is going to get inside the piece and inspect it to uncover all its secrets. By discovering all its secrets, you will be able to really understand what it is all about. Or you might want to think about yourself as the author. If you were the author, what creative writing devices would you use to weave your story? Whether you are a detective or the author, try these strategies to help you understand what you read:

1. Interpreting texts. An author does not always come right out and tell the reader everything. That would make a story boring and too predictable, wouldn't it? Sometimes a writer gives you clues so you can make predictions and try to figure out what comes next. When you are trying to interpret what the author means, keep track of the clues the author is dropping along the way. Continually ask yourself: How do the clues add up? What is this leading to? Am I following the path the author is making for me by following the clues dropped along the way?

2. Monitor comprehension. Continually monitor your understanding. Ask: Do I know what is going on here? If you don't, go back and reread from where you stopped understanding.

3. Get to know the characters. Keep track of how the author is developing the characters. The more you can get inside characters' heads, the more you will be able to understand what motivates them and the more you will be able to predict correctly what might happen next.

4. Word clues. How does the author use words as clues? Are similes used to describe a character or a setting so you can connect it to something you can relate to better? Do signal words hint at when things are happening? If you come across a word you do not know the meaning of, use what you understand about the rest of the passage to help you guess what the word means.

5. Question the reading genre. When you know what to expect from the structure of a genre, it helps you understand what is happening and predict what will come next. For example, if you didn't know that science fiction included adventures based on scientific facts and theories, it might be hard for you to comprehend them.

From the sideline: Tips for Completing the Passage
- *Read all the directions carefully.*
- *Think about the answer before choosing your response.*

Standard 2, Sample Passage A

Directions: **Read this poem that compares a cat and a dog. Answer questions 1 through 3. Note that the numerals to the left represent the line of the poem.**

© Tatiana Morozova

© Tommy Maenhout

CAT AND DOG

1   A cat is like an acrobat
Teetering atop the chair.
A dog is like a clumsy clown
Stumbling everywhere.

5   A cat's purr is like a whisper
Soft and comforting.
A dog's bark is like a siren
Harsh and rattling.

9   A cat is like a proud princess.
A dog is like a rude little child.
A cat's whiskers are tickly feathers.
A dog's tail whips playful and wild.

13   My eyes feast on the perfect cat,
But my heart belongs to the dog.

1. On which literary device does the poet rely **most**?

    A. simile

    B. alliteration

    C. onomatopoeia

    D. metaphor

    *Strategies you used:*_____

2. Which of these phrases, as it is used in the poem, lets the reader know for sure that the author thinks the cat is beautiful?

    A. line 1, "The cat is like an acrobat"

    B. line 5, "The cat's purr is like a whisper"

    C. line 9, "The cat is like a proud princess"

    D. line 13, "My eyes feast on the perfect cat"

    *Strategies you used:*_____

3. How many stanzas are in this poem?

    A. one

    B. two

    C. three

    D. four

    *Strategies you used:*_____

Answers for Sample Passage A

1. The answer is A. While the poet does use some metaphors, the device used most is the simile. Each time she uses the word *like,* she is using a simile. There is no onomatopoeia or alliteration.

2. The answer is D. By using the words *my eyes feast* in the last phrase, the author states outright her personal opinion about the beauty of the cat. Her eyes are satisfied and even overwhelmed by the cat. In the poem the other phrases describe how the cat moves, the sound of its purr, and the attitude of the cat. She doesn't state, however, that these characteristics necessarily mean the cat is beautiful.

3. The answer is D. There are four stanzas in this poem. Stanzas are like the paragraphs of a poem. They are indicated here with an extra line of space between them.

From the sideline: Tips for Completing the Passage
- *Read all the directions carefully.*
- *Think about the answer before choosing your response.*

Standard 2, Sample Passage B

Directions: **Read the following fable about a hungry raccoon. Then answer questions 1 through 3.**

WILEY'S NIGHTTIME SNACK

Written and Illustrated by Dusti Strub

Wiley the raccoon had a busy day. He just finished his work, and now he was ready for a nighttime snack. So, Wiley eagerly walked to the nearest house. He noticed the lights were on, and the humans were still awake. Wiley knew he was not going to be able to pick through the garbage cans to find a delicious snack without being sighted by the humans. Then he noticed the garage door was open and a basket of shiny red apples was stashed in the back corner.

Apples were one of Wiley's favorite nighttime snacks. He could almost taste the sweet juice of the red apples coating his mouth. The apples were shining in Wiley's eyes, and his mouth began to water. All he needed to do was walk quickly past the house and quietly push the basket over to spill the apples. Of course, Wiley had been caught before by humans. But, the thought of the tasty apples was so tempting!

Wiley walked past the window. No one saw him. He darted to the open garage door and put one paw on the cement floor. His motion caused the automatic garage light to turn on, which caused the family dog to start barking. Wiley was startled. The apples were too far back in the garage for him to grab and make a quick escape.

Wiley knew he would not be able to bite his teeth into those juicy apples before the dog would find him. He could hear the barking dog getting closer! He gave the apples one last saddened look before turning around. He said, "I am sure they were overripe, and they had too many worm holes. Or, the humans have not cleaned the harmful pesticides off them yet. I saved myself from getting sick today."

Wiley tucked his tail between his legs and quickly ran away.

1. Why did the author end the fable with the raccoon tucking his tail between his legs and running away?

   A. He hurt his tail while trying to get the apples.

   B. The author wanted to show Wiley felt defeated.

   C. Wiley had been affected by the pesticides.

   D. The author wanted to show Wiley was exhausted from working all day.

   *Strategies you used:*_____

2. Wiley says the apples must be rotten because

   A. he didn't wash the fruit.

   B. of the taste of the pesticide.

   C. he was making an excuse for not getting them.

   D. they were poisoned.

*Strategies you used:*_____

3. Why did Wiley decide to eat apples that day?

   A. The barking dog was getting near.

   B. Apples were one of his favorite nighttime snacks.

   C. He was thirsty.

   D. He ate only fresh fruit.

*Strategies you used:*_____

Answers for Sample Passage B

1. The correct answer is B. There is no suggestion in the fable of Wiley having hurt his tail, having been affected by the pesticides, or being exhausted. We do know, though, that he was making excuses for not being able to get the apples, which implies he had been defeated. Tucking one's tail implies shame or defeat.

2. The correct answer is C. Wiley was making an excuse for not getting the apples. He rationalizes not being able to get them by talking about them being overripe with worm holes and by saying they had harmful pesticides on them.

3. The correct answer is B. The author says this in the second paragraph.

STANDARD 3: LANGUAGE FOR CRITICAL ANALYSIS AND INFORMATION

The questions in Book 1 may test your skills in

- Finding the main idea—Who or what is the passage about? Why did the author write this piece? Who was meant to be the main audience for the passage?

- Using supporting details—What details support the main idea of the passage?

Strategies for Finding the Main Idea

1. If there is a title, it may be a clue to the main idea.
2. The first and/or final paragraphs may state the main idea, or it may be implied by the supporting details in the paragraphs in the middle.
3. Ask: What is the main message the writer is trying to get across?
4. Compare the multiple-choice answers against each other. Usually, a main-idea statement looks different from the others. It does not contain details but rather states broad, general remarks about the passage over-all. For example, the main-idea statement below is choice a.
   a. Bamboo can be used in multiple ways.
   b. Bamboo is found primarily in Asia.
5. As you read, circle supporting details. Then see how they are all connected.
6. Visualize the paragraph in this way:

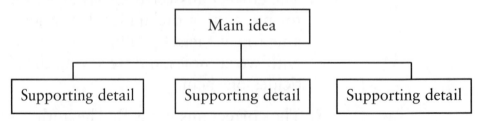

7. Finally, use the multiple-choice tips to decide which choice is the main idea. You might find the process-of-elimination strategy very helpful.

STANDARD 3, SAMPLE PASSAGE A

Think about what you know about finding the main idea, and then review the strategies for finding the main idea and for answering multiple-choice questions in this chapter. Begin by skimming the title, the article, and the questions.

> *From the sideline: Tips for Completing the Passage*
> ■ *Read all the directions carefully.*
> ■ *Think about the answer before choosing your response.*

Directions: **Read the following passage about a challenging marathon run. Then answer questions 1 and 2.**

THE MARATHON OF THE SANDS

Since 1986 the world's greatest and most daring marathon runners have come together in the Sahara Desert. They gather to run in probably the most challenging race in the world, the Marathon of the Sands. This race is the true test of a runner's fitness, ability to overcome challenges, and determination.

This unbelievable foot race covers over 125 miles of mountain wilderness and desert heat. The race takes about seven days for most runners to complete. The athletes run the course carrying everything they need on their backs: food, extra clothing, water, and sleeping bags. It is not a race for the everyday jogger!

Founded by Patrick Bauer, the Marathon of the Sands draws runners from all over the world who find they form lasting friendships with each other. As they tire, they learn a great deal about themselves and each other. They learn how strong their will to continue is and how much they can demand from their minds and bodies.

The challenge of the race includes high temperatures, rough ground, steep hills, dusty and dry air, and running injuries. Each day, the runners must finish between 15 and 18 miles before reaching their camp for the night where they rest to prepare for the next day. On day one, they run 15 miles across rocks and thorn bushes. On day two, they run through 18 miles of 100+ degree heat. On the third day, the runners climb steep sand dunes while dust and sweat cake their bodies. The fourth and fifth days are reported to be the worst as they cross miles of rocks and dunes in 125-degree temperatures. Many runners needing medical help are rescued at this point by helicopters. On the sixth day, the wind picks up in the Valley of Dra. Finally, on the last day, after running the final 12 miles, finishers are greeted by friends and others as they complete the race.

The Marathon of the Sands is a challenge that will test even the greatest of athletes' limits. It is not a race against time. It is a race against the desert and a runner's determination and ability to finish something they started.

1. Which of the following is the main idea of this passage?

   A. The marathoners run seven days and six nights through the desert.

   B. Patrick Bauer founded the Marathon of the Sands.

   C. The Marathon of the Sands is a 125-mile foot race in the Sahara Desert.

   D. The Marathon of the Sands tests runners' fitness and determination.

   *Strategies you used:*_____

2. Which statement is supported by information in the article?

   A. Most people who begin the marathon do not finish it.

   B. No woman has ever finished this race.

   C. Each night runners rest and prepare for the next day's run.

   D. The Sahara Desert is the hottest desert in the world.

   *Strategies you used:*_____

Answers for Sample Passage A

1. The main idea is D. Choices A and B are minor details. You may have been tempted by choice C, but D gives a broader overall picture of the passage by including the challenges the runners face. If you drew a visual representation of the passage, you might have done this:

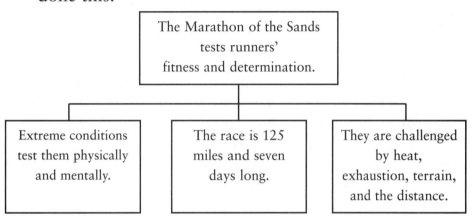

2. By using the process of elimination and checking back in the passage, you will agree that the correct answer here is C. The reader is told the race is broken into a certain number of miles each day and that the runners carry their sleeping bags with them. The reader is not told what percentage of runners completes the marathon. Readers are also not told whether women enter or complete the marathon. When asked what the passage supports, respond based only on what you have learned directly from the passage. For example, you may think the Sahara Desert is the hottest desert in the world. This is not stated or supported by the passage, though.

> *From the sideline: Tips for Completing the Passage*
> ▪ *Read all the directions carefully.*
> ▪ *Think about the answer before choosing your response.*

Standard 3, Sample Passage B

Directions: Read this excerpt of a personal narrative about a game called roundball that is written in a dialect. Then answer questions 1 and 2.

CITRUS HOOPS

Ryan Curry

To many, Citrus is just an elementary school located at Citrus and 4th Avenue, but to many others it's the ultimate place to play roundball. The three full courts all have baskets of different heights: one at eight feet, one at eight and a half, and one at nine and a half. From dawn to dusk on weekends and from 3:00 to 8:00 on weekdays, games are played. In Chico, there is no better place to hoop.

But before you decide to go play at Citrus, ya gotta have an understanding. If you're new, you're gonna have to prove yourself. And if people start talkin' about Sir Ronald, understand that Sir Ronald is the only man known to have completed a Double Dip. No, it's not at Baskin-Robbins. A Double Dip is when a player dunks the ball and before it hits the ground takes it out of the air and dunks it again. Understand and respect the veterans, and you'll stand a chance.

I finish lacing my shoes, step through the wire fence and call "winners." Everybody looks and nobody argues. When you're a Citrus veteran no-no-noooobody will mess with ya.

Credit: Jack Rawlins/*The Writer's Way*/Copyright©1996/by Houghton Mifflin Company

1. This passage is mostly about
   A. a young man's pride in being a veteran roundball player.
   B. how to play roundball.
   C. how to complete a "Double Dip."
   D. regulation basket heights for roundball.

   *Strategies you used:*_____

2. Which statement is supported by information in the article?

   A. You have to earn respect from others at Citrus to be accepted.

   B. Only veteran roundball players are allowed to play at Citrus.

   C. Only students who go to Citrus can play roundball on its courts.

   D. Special shoes are needed to play at Citrus.

   *Strategies you used:*_____

Answers for Sample Passage B

1. The correct answer is A. Although choices B, C, and D are included in the passage, they are details in the story. Choice A provides the overall main idea of the narrative because many details link to and support it.

2. The correct answer is A. The passage says "you're gonna have to prove yourself" and when you're a veteran, nobody will mess with you. Choices B, C, and D are never mentioned in the passage the way they are stated in the question. The passage does talk about these points, but it does not say what the choices say.

For more practice in finding the main idea and supporting details, go to the Online Resources section.

SCORING

In this multiple-choice part of the State test, you will get credit for each question you answer correctly. Answers left blank receive no credit, so it is better to make a careful, thoughtful guess than to leave a blank.

ONLINE RESOURCES

Kids' Lab Main Idea Practice Page *www.manatee.k12. fl.us/sites/elementary/palmasola/rcmiprac1.htm*

Kids' Lab Main Idea Tutorial *www.manatee.k12.fl.us/ sites/elementary/palmasola/rcmi1.htm*

Harcourt What's the Big Idea? *www.harcourtschool.com/ activity/book_buddy/rosie/skill_pre.html*

These web sites offer fun learning games and lots of practice in finding the main idea. You can even take quizzes to see how well you are doing.

CONGRATULATIONS!

Now you know what Book 1 is all about. You have read about the parts of the test, the test directions, and the question breakdown. You have also learned a number of strategies for

▪ answering multiple-choice questions,

▪ collecting information from your reading,

▪ responding to literature, and

▪ finding the main idea

while you practiced sample questions from the test.

Next, you should continue on to Chapter 4. There, you will learn all about Book 2 of the State test.

BOOK 2: LISTENING AND WRITING

DESCRIPTION

What is Book 2 all about? Book 2 is the listening and writing section of the State test. In this section, you will

- carefully listen to a story read two times,
- take notes while you listen, and
- write short responses and extended responses to several questions.

There will be four questions to answer for a total of 5 points. The first involves completing a graphic organizer of some kind. You have probably created t-charts and webs before to help you organize your thoughts about a reading. The next two questions will ask you to comprehend and interpret what you heard by writing short answers of about four or five sentences each. The fourth question requires a longer response. You will answer this question by using several examples and details from the story to support your response.

Remember, this part of the State test checks your listening comprehension. When you answer the questions, base your responses solely on the passage you heard read to you, not on your opinion or feelings about the topic. Enter the world of the story as you learned to do in Chapter 1.

The teacher will take about 15 minutes to prepare you to take the test. After you have gone through the directions with your teacher, he or she will read the passage to you two times. You will take notes. Then you will be given 45 minutes to answer the four questions in Book 2. During that time, you will work independently without help and without speaking to your classmates. At any time during your writing, you may look back to check your notes.

TEST DIRECTIONS

Your teacher will pass out Book 2. It includes three short-response questions and one extended-response question. There will be spaces for you to write your responses after each question. You will write directly in the test booklet using a no. 2 pencil. You may print or write in cursive. Whichever you use, be sure it is clear and easy to read.

There are no separate answer sheets. You will not use separate scrap paper for notes or for drafting your responses. Only the responses written in the test booklet will be scored as part of the test. If you run out of room on the pages in the booklet for your answers, you may use any other blank pages inside the booklet. Just be sure to clearly and very carefully label where you have continued your response so the person scoring your test will be able to easily recognize and find it. Do not continue one answer into the space meant for the answer to another question.

To begin, your teacher will go over the directions with you. You will read some tips for taking the test, such as

■ read the directions carefully;

■ be sure to organize your time so you have enough time to plan, write, revise, and proofread your responses; and

■ think about the questions and your responses before writing.

Next, you will read about how to check your writing. This is a very important step in doing well on this part of the test. Maybe it is not your favorite thing to do, but proofreading can make a world of difference in helping a reader understand what you have written. And, with all the effort you have put into expressing your thoughts, you want your reader to be able to enjoy it and walk away saying, "What great ideas!" Your teacher does not correct or score the writing passages. They are sent to educators who do not know you. See Check Your Writing in the strategies chart in this chapter for tips on revising and proofreading your work.

TESTING ACCOMMODATIONS

The directions that are read to all students and the section on listening may be read aloud. If a student's IEP or 504 Plan indicates the test may be read, all the other directions and the questions may also be read to the student. Students may not use spell checkers or grammar checkers or have requirements for writing mechanics such as spelling and punctuation waived for them. See the *School Administrator's Manual* at *http://www.emsc.nysed.gov/osa* for more information on accommodations.

BREAKDOWN OF QUESTIONS

Book 2 focuses on Standard 2 of the New York State Grade 6 English Language Arts test. That is, are you able to read, write, listen, and speak for literary response and expression? The answer to question 30 in Book 2, the extended-response question, is also used as part of the writing mechanics score.

GETTING STARTED

Next, you will learn strategies for listening, taking notes, and writing short and extended responses to questions about a story you have just been read two times.

As you work through this chapter, think

What do I already do when I listen, take notes, and write?

Start with what you know and what works for you already. Then read our suggestions to add to your strategies. Here we go!

STUDENT CHECKLISTS OF STRATEGIES TO USE

Use these checklists, which describe many strategies you could use to best answer the practice questions in the following sections. After each question, write down which strategies helped you. This will help you remember what strategies you should use.

CHECKLIST OF STRATEGIES FOR LISTENING

_____ Be an active listener. Focus on what the reader is saying.

_____ Try to visualize (get a picture of) the story as you are listening. Where are the characters? What do they look like? What are they doing?

_____ Put yourself inside the story. Think of yourself as one of the characters or think about how the characters get along with each other.

_____ Look right at the reader's face. This will help you focus and avoid distractions.

_____ Imagine your ears have grown twice their size and are absorbing the story.

_____ During the first reading, focus on the structure and content of the story.

_____ During the second reading, focus on the supporting details.

CHECKLIST OF STRATEGIES FOR COMPLETING SHORT-RESPONSE QUESTIONS

_____ Read the question carefully. Review your notes. Reread the question. Think about your response.

_____ Budget your time. Save most of your time for the final question since it requires a longer answer. Do not spend more than 15 minutes on the three short responses.

_____ Proofread! Proofread! Proofread! Check for grammar, punctuation, spelling, and organization.

_____ After you finish proofreading, read the question one last time. Does your response actually answer the question? Does it say what you want it to say?

CHECKLIST OF STRATEGIES FOR COMPLETING EXTENDED-RESPONSE QUESTIONS

Take Detailed Notes

_____ Remember you have two shots at taking helpful notes. When you miss something the first time, do not get frazzled. Mark the spot you missed with a big X and try to fill it in during the second reading.

_____ Do not try to write out complete sentences. Write just enough so that you will understand what you meant.

_____ Make use of marks and spacing between words and phrases to organize your notes. For example, use dots or bullets to show items on a list. Use arrows to show cause and effect.

_____ Make use of your own kind of shorthand. Use symbols, abbreviations, or drawings.

_____ Take a minute to go back through your notes right away to fill in missing information or reorganize ideas.

Plan Your Writing

_____ Spend just a few minutes organizing the big ideas and the sequence of your answer.

_____ Write an outline, draw a graphic organizer, or jot down some notes.

_____ Now is the time to plan the paragraphing and the overall structure of the essay.

_____ Do NOT write a complete draft of your response on the planning page. This will take too much time.

_____ Make use of your own kind of shorthand here also by using symbols, abbreviations, or drawings to save time.

Write the Essay

_____ Include an introductory paragraph. This paragraph should briefly answer the question.

_____ Write a second paragraph that explains the answer by describing two or three examples, details, or actions from the story and your notes that support the answer.

_____ Write a third paragraph that elaborates on the answer and includes connections with what you know about the topic beyond the story. Don't go crazy here, though. You do not want to distract your reader and wander off the topic.

_____ Write a short final paragraph that ties it all up and restates your simple answer to the question from the introduction.

_____ Use transitional words between paragraphs and thoughts. Words like _first, before, then, finally, next, consequently, in addition, therefore, ordinarily, generally,_ and _above all_ help to smooth out and organize an essay.

Check Your Writing

_____ Check the content. Repeatedly check that you are answering the question and using details right from the story and your notes to support your responses. Ask: Did I answer the question to the very best of my ability?

_____ Check the organization and flow of your writing. Is it sequenced and logical?

_____ Take the reader's place. Are you putting yourself to sleep as you read your response? Then you are probably boring your reader, too. Make your writing interesting.

_____ Check the mechanics several times. One time, check for spelling; another time, check for capitalization and punctuation. Another time, check for sentence fragments and run-on sentences. (Remember, the answer to question 30 is used as part of your writing mechanics score.)

_____ Be sure to check for the kinds of errors you usually make when you write. We all have areas we are unsure of in writing. Pay special attention to them in your final read.

SAMPLE QUESTIONS WITH GUIDED PRACTICE

In this section, there is a practice listening selection. That means you will need help in this chapter. Ask a skillful, fluent reader to assist you by reading this section to you.

Note to Reader: Take the story "A Shared Dream" out of the book by cutting on the perforation marks. That way, the student can use the Notes pages to take notes in the book while you are reading.

The reader should practice reading the story on his or her own first and then read the selection TO you TWICE. When the person reads, he or she should begin with the title and the name of the author. Then, the reader should read the selection at a steady and moderate pace—not too fast and not to slowly. The reader should speak in a clear voice and read with expression. Remember, the selection should be read two times. Each reading should take about five minutes.

From the sideline: As you work through this guided practice, check these "From the Sideline" features to monitor your thinking. Use the strategies in these features as guides to help you answer each question successfully. Check off each item as you monitor it.

Directions: **You will hear a story called "A Shared Dream" by Julia Baxter-MacGregor. You will listen to the story two times. You may take notes at any time as you listen to the story. Then you will use your notes to help you answer the questions that follow. Your answers to these questions will show your understanding of the story.**

NOTES

NOTES

A SHARED DREAM

Julia Baxter-MacGregor

Martha ran breathlessly through the darkness. She knew she had one chance to see her friend before he would be gone from her life forever. In her hands she carried a coat, socks, and a small bundle of food. "Would it be enough?" she asked herself. As she ran, she kept looking over her shoulder to be sure she wasn't being followed. All she saw behind her was the moon, as bright and full as the silver platters her meals were served on in the big house. Martha felt her heart pounding in her chest, like someone knocking to get out of a room in which they did not want to be.

She was completely out of breath now, from both fear and the pace at which she was running. She knew that if she was caught, it would mean big trouble for both herself and her friend. As she stopped to lean on a tree and watched the leaves cast dancing shadows on the forest floor, she began to cry. She knew that her friend's only chance to be really happy meant that he had to go away, but she would miss him. For the last ten years, they had played together in the fields, pretending to be frogs and butterflies. He taught her songs that he and his family sang while working in the fields, and she taught him the songs she learned at church on Sundays. But mostly, they shared dreams. They shared dreams that they could one day be the kind of friends who could walk down the streets of Charleston together, and that no one would care. Deep in her heart, she knew this could never happen, and the longing for it made the tears come even faster.

Gathering her strength, she set off again for the clearing in which she knew she would find her friend and his family. Time stood still. She kept running and could hear her feet crunching the leaves below them, but she felt as if she were standing still. Finally, she saw her destination. It was a clearing in the woods. There, under the canopy of a big tree, was her friend. His black face was shining in the moonlight, and she could see both fear and hope reflected in his dark eyes. She ran to him, dropping her bundles on the ground, and threw her arms around him. For what seemed like forever, they cried in each other's arms.

Finally, Martha looked at him and said, "Andy, you need to go now. I know it won't be long before someone on the plantation finds you all missing. Here are some things I hope will help you on your journey."

Andy took the bundles and smiled. "You be a good friend, Martha," he whispered. "I gonna miss you."

Martha smiled and grabbed his hand one last time. She knew she would never hold her friend's hand again. Looking around at his family, she smiled at them. They smiled back at her, not wanting to talk, for fear of making any noise. In their faces she saw the dreams Andy had shared with her. Dreams of freedom. With a nod of his head, Andy's father beckoned the family into the forest beyond. In what seemed like the blink of an eye, they were gone.

When Martha arrived back at her house, she sat in her bedroom looking out the window. In the sky she saw the stars she knew they were following to the first safe place. She wondered if Andy was looking at them, too. In her heart, she knew he was, and that, somehow, made her feel like they were still connected. As she finally got into bed, she hoped that Andy and his family would find their way to the North and to the free life they longed for. With this dream she shared with Andy in her heart, she fell asleep.

Strategies you used for listening: _____

_____

Strategies you used for taking notes: _____

_____

SHORT-RESPONSE QUESTIONS

1. Fill in the following chart. Provide one word to describe how Martha most likely feels about her friend Andy leaving. Next, describe an action included in the story that supports this feeling.

> *From the sideline: What is the question asking?*
> ■ *Underline phrases that focus in on what you should include in your answer.*

How Martha Most Likely Feels	An Action or Detail Included in the Story That Supports This Feeling

> *From the sideline: In your answer, be sure you*
> ■ *choose one "feeling" word and*
> ■ *describe one action or detail from the story to support your answer.*

Strategies you used: _____

2. Explain how Martha's feelings about Andy leaving compare to Andy's feelings about leaving. Use details from the story to support your answer.

> *From the sideline: What is the question asking?*
> ■ *Underline phrases that focus in on what you should include in your answer.*

_____

_____

_____

_____

_____

_____

_____

> *From the sideline: Be sure your answer*
> ■ *describes Martha's feelings and Andy's feelings,*
> ■ *gives details from the story to support that these are their feelings, and*
> ■ *compares Martha's feelings with Andy's feelings.*

*Strategies you used:*_____

3. What clues does the author give the reader to explain the setting, who Andy and his family are, and why they are running away? Use details from the story and your notes to support your answer.

From the sideline: What is the question asking?
■ *Underline phrases that focus in on what you should include in your answer.*

_____

_____

_____

_____

_____

_____

_____

From the sideline: Be sure your answer
■ *describes the setting,*
■ *tells who Andy and his family are,*
■ *tells why they are running away, and*
■ *includes two or three clues from the story to support your understandings.*

---

*Strategies you used:*_____

EXTENDED-RESPONSE QUESTION

Planning Page

Use this page to PLAN your writing for question 4. Do NOT write your final answer here. Anything you write on the planning page will NOT count toward your final score. Write your FINAL answer on the lines that follow the question.

> *From the sideline: Your planning page could consist of*
> ▪ *a graphic organizer to illustrate the organization of your essay;*
> ▪ *these parts of your essay—*
>   • *Introduction,*
>   • *Supporting details,*
>   • *Connections,*
>   • *Conclusion; and*
> ▪ *well-organized notes sequencing several paragraphs and bulleting details within each paragraph.*

PLAN here.

Continue to PLAN here.

> *From the sideline: Check.*
> ■ *Does your plan focus on answering the question? Reread the question to be sure. If so, continue. If not, go back and revise to refocus.*

4. In this story, Martha and Andy share a dream. Write an essay explaining what that dream is. Use details from the story to support your answer.

> *From the sideline: What is the question asking?*
> ■ *Underline phrases that focus in on what you should include in your answer.*

_____

_____

_____

_____

_____

_____

_____

_____

_____

_____

_____

_____

_____

_____

_____

_____

_____

_____

From the sideline: Check.
■ *Are you still focused on answering the question? If so, continue. If not, go back and revise to refocus.*

> *From the sideline: Be sure your essay answers the question. Does it*
> ■ *Explain the shared dream?*
> ■ *Provide several details from the story that support that this is the dream they share?*
> ■ *Show a rich understanding of the full meaning of the story?*
> ■ *Include some connections beyond the text without giving your opinion about the issue or topic?*
> ■ *Have an introduction and conclusion?*
>
> *Have you checked your spelling, punctuation, paragraphing, capitalization, grammar, and language use? (The answer to the extended-response question is the question in Book 2 that is used as part of your writing mechanics score.)*

Strategies you used: _____

_____

SCORING

Now, let's look at how your responses will be scored in Book 2. After you read through this section, go back and improve your responses before you check the sample answers at the end of this chapter.

Your responses will be scored in five areas: meaning, development, organization, language use, and conventions (writing mechanics). See Appendix C for two sample scoring rubrics. Use the Grade 6 English Language Arts Rubric Chart to score the four responses in Book 2 for meaning, development, organization, and language use—the first four areas. Each question is not scored separately but as a cluster or group. You will get from 0 to 5 points on the cluster of questions as a whole. The fifth area, conventions, is scored using the Writing Mechanics Rubric Chart, which is also found in Appendix C. On the test, the extended responses in Books 2 and 3 are scored together. You can get 0 to 3 points for conventions.

Now that you know how the scoring works, let's take a look at what each area on the rubrics includes.

1. Meaning: Does your answer show you understand the story and how to answer the questions? To get the top score, you should
   a. completely answer the questions,
   b. show you understand and can interpret the ideas and the topic or theme of the story, and
   c. connect the story to other things you know.
2. Development: Is your answer strong? To get the top score, you should
   a. express your ideas thoroughly and elaborate with details and
   b. pull relevant examples from the story to show you completely understand.
3. Organization: Is your writing structured and easy to follow? To get the top score, you should
   a. be focused and stick to the point and the plan to express your thoughts,
   b. sequence your ideas so they make sense, and
   c. use transitions between paragraphs and ideas.
4. Language use: Is your language interesting and intelligent? To get the top score, you should
   a. write in a way that flows easily, engages the reader, and rouses interest;
   b. use interesting vocabulary such as vivid adjectives and descriptive adverbs that show a high level of vocabulary knowledge and use; and
   c. vary the way you structure your sentences.
5. Conventions: How are your grammar, punctuation, and spelling? To get the top score, you should
   a. proofread very carefully so that you have very few, if any, errors;
   b. check all grammar, capitalization, punctuation, and sentence structure;
   c. separate your essay into paragraphs appropriately; and
   d. especially check conventions in the extended-response question because this is the response used as part of your writing mechanics score. See Appendix C for the Writing Mechanics Rubric Chart.

After reading the Scoring section, go back to the guided practice questions in this book and see what you can do to improve your answers and your writing. Then look at the possible responses that are given next. Would you give yourself the top score for this cluster of four questions? Would you give yourself the top score for conventions in the extended response? If not, why not? It's a good idea, too, to ask someone else to look over your responses and score them using the rubrics in Appendix C. They may notice things you did not, and they may be able to give you some helpful suggestions for improving your responses and writing. Think about which parts of the Scoring section you could improve on even more when you get to the two practice tests in Chapters 6 and 7.

SAMPLE NOTES

Here is an example of how you might take notes for "A Shared Dream." You want to note the main ideas of the story and details to support these ideas. Using a t-chart like the one used here can be an effective way of organizing your thoughts as you listen to the story. The notes in black are notes taken during the first reading. The notes in blue were added during the second reading. Notice that the notes for the first reading are more general. The reader was listening to the whole story to understand the beginning, middle, and ending. She wanted to know who the characters were and what roles they played in the story, what the setting was, and what the general sequence and tone of the story was. Many details were added during the second reading. This way the listener was able to grasp a full understanding of the story and to note many details that she would be able to use in writing her essay.

Story Notes	Details
Martha running to meet friend	darkness
friend leaving forever	
bringing supplies	coat, socks + food
being followed?	afraid, heart pounding
rich?	silver platters, big house
trouble if caught	for her + friend
Martha will miss friend	his only chance to be happy
grew up together	play in fields, pretend + sing, his fam work fields; M to church
shared dream: walk together w/no one caring	streets of Charleston; M knew "deep in her heart" would never happen
Meets friend + his fam	black face, dark eyes, fear/hope in eyes
hugs him, both cry	"for what seemed like forever"
M: you need to go	before found missing—Andy a slave?
gives supplies	A: you be a good friend, M. I gonna miss you
M grabs hand	will never hold again
M smile at fam	smile back not want to talk (noise)—dreams in faces
Dreams of freedom in faces	leave into woods—blink of an eye
M goes home, looks out window	
Stars connect M + A	
M hopes A + fam find North	+ free life
M falls asleep	with dream shared w/A in her heart

Notice the use of symbols, abbreviations, and incomplete sentences. The + symbol stands for *and*. And "fam" stands for *family*. M and A represent the characters' names, Martha and Andy. The only punctuation used is to separate thoughts or to show direct quotes. A few times direct quotes are shown by just writing who is speaking with a colon after the abbreviation for the character's name, such as "M: you need to go." When the note taker writes her essay, she will have excellent details to support her answer. These quotes will really add voice and interest for her readers.

Finally, notice that several times during her note taking, this person asks herself some questions. For example, she writes "rich?" and "Andy a slave?" These are not stated in the story. As she was listening, these questions came to mind. She wrote them down to help her organize her thinking.

POSSIBLE RESPONSES TO THE SAMPLE QUESTIONS IN THIS CHAPTER

Short-Response Questions

Question 1. Fill in the following chart. Provide one word describing how Martha most likely feels about her friend Andy leaving. Next, describe an action included in the story that supports this feeling.

Possible Response

How Martha Most Likely Feels	An Action or Detail Included in the Story That Supports This Feeling
sad	Martha threw her arms around Andy and cried for what seemed like forever

Other Possible Responses:

- Fearful—She was out of breath from both fear and the pace at which she was running.
- Worried/anxious/apprehensive—She leaned up against a tree and cried.
- Lonely/forlorn—She knew Andy had to go away but she would miss him.
- Melancholy—She remembered playing with Andy in the fields.
- Hopeful—She dreamed they could one day walk down the streets together and no one would care.
- Connected—She looked at the stars and wondered if Andy was looking at the same stars.
- Tired/exhausted—She had been running and at the end fell asleep.

Notice that the action or detail is an event or comment right from the story. Be sure not to include information you know from outside the story here. Take the information right from the story.

Question 2. Explain how Martha's feelings about Andy leaving compare to Andy's feelings about leaving. Use details from the story to support your answer.

Possible Response

We know that Martha was feeling very sad about Andy leaving because she was crying and hugging him. She has sneaked out of the house to meet him in the woods and bring him some supplies for his journey. Andy was sad, too, because he had been friends with Martha and they had played together in the fields. Now they would never see each other again. The story says Martha knew she would never hold her friend's hand

*again. While they both felt sad, we know that Andy was also
fearful and hopeful. Martha saw fear and hope reflected in
Andy's eyes. He had shared his dreams of freedom with her.*

Again, state only information you learned from the story.

*Question 3. What clues does the author give the reader to
explain the setting, who Andy and his family are, and why
they are running away? Use details from the story and
your notes to support your answer.*

Possible Response

*The story takes place in the South in the United States during
the time of slavery. We know this because the author talks
about Andy and his family working in the plantation fields, the
big house, and dreams of freedom. We know Andy and his
family are slaves because they have to run away from the
plantation to get their freedom. They are worried about being
caught, so they don't talk. We also know Andy and Martha
shared dreams about being the kind of friends who could walk
down the streets of Charleston with no one caring. Charleston is
a city in the South. Finally, Andy's black face shined in the
moonlight.*

Here again, be sure to only state information and details
that came from the story. For example, you cannot say
that Martha's family owned Andy and his family as slaves
because the story never says that.

Extended-Response Question

Question 4. In this story, Martha and Andy share a dream. Write an essay to explain what that dream is. Use details from the story to support your answer.

First, you will plan your essay. You are given two blank pages to do this. Here are two examples of how you might quickly organize your essay. In this outline the main items (I, II, III, and IV) would each be a separate paragraph. The letters under each numeral would include your supporting details from the story.

Outline style:

    I. *Introduction*

        A. *dream of freedom*

        B. *equality*

        C. *who M + A are*

    II. *Supporting details*

        A. *describe meeting + feelings*

        B. *A's chance to be happy*

        C. *shared dream of being friends*

        D. *Charleston streets*

   III. *Connections*

        A. *running away*

        B. *Underground RR*

   IV. *Conclusion*

T-chart:

As the note taker did, you could use a t-chart to organize your notes into an essay structure.

Paragraphs	Details
Intro	dream of freedom
	equality
	Who M + A are
Details	describe meeting + feelings
	A's chance to be happy
	shared dream of being friends
	Charleston streets
Connections	running away
	Underground RR
Conclusion	

Now, we are ready to look at an example of how these notes and planning helped create a solid, organized essay.

Possible Response

In "A Shared Dream," Martha and Andy share a dream of freedom and equality for slaves. Martha is a young girl whose family lives on a plantation in the South during the time of slavery. Andy and his family are slaves.

In this story, Martha gathers a coat, socks, and some food. She sneaks out of the house and runs to a clearing in the woods. Here she meets Andy and his family who are preparing to run away into the woods and to the first safe house on their way to freedom. Martha knows Andy's only chance to be happy means he has to run away from the plantation toward freedom. They both have dreamed about one day being the kind of friends who could walk down the streets of Charleston with no one caring. This shows they have dreamed of equality between slaves and their owners. Martha is afraid Andy will be caught. She says it won't be long before someone finds them missing. This is because slaves were at that time considered the property of their plantation owners. If they were caught running away, they were returned to their owners. They were not free to go where they wanted to go.

In other readings about slavery, I have learned that many slaves did try to run away. While some were caught and severely beaten or whipped, others found their freedom. Many people, especially Northerners, helped slaves achieve their freedom. A trail called the Underground Railroad was a well-known way for slaves to run to the North and their freedom. Many people shared Martha and Andy's dream for freedom and equality between black and white people.

Martha and Andy share a dream. Many others through history have shared the same dream. Many still work toward achieving equality among races. They, too, have a dream.

ONLINE RESOURCES

The Homework Center's Listening Skills *http://www. infoplease.com/homework/listeningskills1.html*
What does it mean to really listen? Read the bulleted list on this web page for good tips.

What Is Listening? *http://www.ccsf.edu/Services/LAC/ lern10/listening.html*
This site is from the Learning Assistance Center. It describes what good listeners and poor listeners do.

CONGRATULATIONS!

Now you know what Book 2 is all about. You have read about the parts of the test, the test directions, and the question breakdown. You have also learned a number of strategies for

- listening,
- answering short-response questions,
- answering extended-response questions,
- taking notes,
- planning your writing,
- writing essays, and
- checking your writing

while you practiced sample questions from the test.
Next, you should continue on to Chapter 5. There, you will learn all about the final book of the State test, Book 3.

BOOK 3: READING AND WRITING

DESCRIPTION

What is Book 3 all about? Book 3 is the reading and writing section of the State test. In this section, you will be given two different passages to read. You will apply the reading and writing skills you have learned in class and in this book by answering short- and extended-response questions based on Standard 3. Your answers will show what you understand about the passages, but your answers must also express your opinion, ideas, and thoughts as you critically analyze, compare, and contrast the readings. Critical analysis involves judging or expressing an opinion about what you have read. Your opinions and judgments should be based on details from the reading as they relate to your personal experiences.

In this section, you will

- critically read a passage and answer two short-response questions about it;
- critically read a second passage and answer a short-response question about it; and
- write an extended response to a final question that evaluates, compares, or contrasts the two passages.

There will be two reading passages and four questions to answer. The questions are worth a total of 5 points. You will read the first passage. The first question involves completing a **graphic organizer** of some kind about the first passage. You have surely created t-charts and webs before to help you organize your thoughts. (See the Online Resources section of this chapter for examples of several kinds of graphic organizers.) The graphic organizer most commonly used on the State test in the past, however, has been the t-chart. T-charts help you organize events or ideas into categories. See Figures 5.1 and 5.2.

Fruits	Vegetables
Peaches	Peppers
Pears	Squash

Figure 5.1   A Simple Two-Category T-Chart

Type of Animal	Habitat (Where It Lives)	How Habitat Protects
Lion	Jungle	Provides coverage
Chipmunk	Underground (holes)	Provides safety from predators

Figure 5.2   A Simple Three-Category T-Chart

Then you will answer a short-response question about the first reading. Next, you will read the second passage and answer another short-response question about that. Finally, the fourth question will require a longer response and critical thinking about the readings. You will answer this question by using several examples and details from both stories to support your thoughts about a topic connected to the readings. You might be asked to compare what is similar in the articles and contrast what is different. Then you will support your responses with details from both passages.

Remember, Book 3 focuses on the English Language Arts Standard 3. That is, are you able to read, write, and listen for critical analysis and evaluation? When you answer the questions, you will base your responses not only on the information in the passages you read but also on your opinion, evaluation, and personal experiences with the topic. You will not be scored on whether the scorer thinks your personal opinion is right or wrong, though.

After the teacher has gone over the directions with you, you will be given 60 minutes to answer the four questions in Book 3. During that time, you will work independently without help and without speaking to your classmates. At any time during your writing, you may look back to reread the passages.

TEST DIRECTIONS

Your teacher will pass out Book 3. There will be spaces to write your responses after each question. You will write directly in the booklet using a no. 2 pencil. You may print or write in cursive. Whichever you use, be sure it is clear and easy to read.

There are no separate answer sheets. You will not use separate scrap paper for notes or for drafting your responses. Only the responses written in the test book will be scored as part of the test. If you run out of room on the pages in the booklet for your answers, you may use any other blank pages inside the booklet. Just be sure to clearly and very carefully label where you have continued your response so the person scoring your test will be able to easily recognize and find it. Do not continue one answer into the space meant for an answer to another question.

To begin, your teacher will go over the directions with you. You will read some tips for taking the test, such as

- read the directions carefully;
- be sure to organize your time so you have enough time to plan, write, revise, and proofread your responses; and

■ think about the questions and your responses before writing.

Next, you will read about how to check your writing. In Book 3 you should be sure to

■ organize and express your ideas very clearly;

■ answer the questions fully and accurately;

■ give several examples to support your ideas;

■ make your writing engaging and interesting to the reader; and

■ use paragraphs with correct spelling, punctuation, and grammar.

These points are very important in doing well on this part of the test. See Check Your Writing in Chapter 4 for tips on revising and proofreading your work.

TESTING ACCOMMODATIONS

If you are a student with a disability or you have an individualized education program (IEP), you may be eligible for testing accommodations. For Book 3, because it measures how well you understand what you read, only the directions—no other parts of the book—may be read aloud to you. Your teacher will be sure you are given any accommodations you are allowed.

BREAKDOWN OF QUESTIONS

The questions in Book 3 are all based on ELA Standard 3 on critical analysis and evaluation. The answer to question 34 in Book 3, the extended response, is also used as part of the writing mechanics score.

GETTING STARTED

Next, you will learn strategies for critically analyzing and evaluating passages. As you work through this chapter, think

How do I already analyze or form judgments about what I read?

Start with what you know and what already works for you. Then read our suggestions to add to your strategies. Here we go!

STUDENT CHECKLIST OF STRATEGIES TO USE

Use these checklists, which describe many strategies you could use to best answer the practice questions in the following section. Also, look at the Checklist of Strategies in Chapters 3 and 4 to help you comprehend the readings and organize your writing. After each question, write down which strategies helped you. This will help you remember what strategies you should use.

CHECKLIST OF STRATEGIES FOR CRITICAL ANALYSIS

_____ Read with a pencil. As you read, underline the most important ideas. In the margins write brief questions or comments. Use punctuation marks such as ! and ? to bring attention to interesting or questionable parts of the passage. When you make a connection to a personal experience, put the letter C for *connection* in the margin.

_____ Ask yourself, What is the main idea of the passage? Or summarize the passage in your mind in just one sentence. Do I agree or disagree with this idea?

_____ Decide what you think the author's opinion is. How does it compare or contrast with your personal opinion?

_____ After you've decided what your opinion is, go back into the passage and put a star next to three or four details that will help you support your opinion.

SAMPLE QUESTIONS WITH GUIDED PRACTICE

From the sideline: As you work through this guided practice, check the "From the Sideline" features to monitor your thinking. Use the strategies in these features as guides to help you answer each question successfully. Check off each item as you monitor it.

Directions: In Book 3 you will read an article called "Fossils and Earth's History" and another article called "Cleaning Up the World" about an environmental scientist's work. You will write answers to four questions based on your reading. You may look back at the articles as frequently as you want.

FOSSILS AND EARTH'S HISTORY

Linda Pratt and J. Michael Pratt

Animals and plants have lived on earth for millions of years. Animals that lived in the sea were buried in mud and sand when they died. When plants living in swamps died, they also became buried in mud or sand. The mud and sand slowly hardened and, after a very long time, turned into rock. Little by little, the dead animals and plants inside the rock became fossils. Fossils are the preserved remains of animals and plants that died millions of years ago. So, when we find rocks made of mud or sand, sometimes they have fossils in them.

   Fossils can be very helpful in telling us about past life, climate, geology, and environments and how plants and animals adapted to changes in climate and environment. They can show where animals and plants once lived. The most common fossils are animals that lived in oceans. If you know where to look, fossils of plants that grew in swamps are also easy to find. Also, did you know that the coal we burn for heat is fossil plants?

© Jakez

Today, scientists study fossils to see what animals and plants looked like and how they survived millions of years ago. Most fossils look like some of the plants and animals that are alive today. By comparing fossils with what is living today, scientists learn many facts. They learn how animals and plants on earth long ago may have gradually changed into the animal and plant life that we see today. For example, the crocodiles of today are descendants of the SuperCroc of long ago. Fossils also can give clues about how animals moved. They also can show what animals ate or how they protected themselves. Did you know that dinosaur footprints can tell us how fast various species of dinosaurs ran and if they lived alone or in groups? Learning about the animals of the past can help us protect the animals and people of today's world.

Scientists also study fossils to learn when and how the earth changed. Long ago the earth was very different from what we see today. The five continents that we see on a globe were once part of one giant landmass that broke apart. Each large chunk of land then moved around very slowly like a block of wood in water. Fossils found today in different parts of the world tell us where the continents were long ago.

Finding fossils is almost like looking for buried treasure. Sometimes you can find a fossil that no one else has ever seen before. Collecting fossils and studying them is a great hobby for anyone, and it does not cost much money. You can share your collection with family and friends. And you can learn many things about how animals, plants, and the earth have changed over time.

So, the next time you look at a rock, look at it carefully. You may find a fossil—a fossil of an animal or plant that lived millions of years ago. What secrets does it hold about the past and what can it teach us about the future?

Strategies you used for comprehending and reading critically: _____

_____

_____

SHORT-RESPONSE QUESTIONS

1. The authors of "Fossils and Earth's History" describe several different things fossils tell us about the earth's history. Complete the chart below by identifying one reason scientists study fossils and what they do with this information. Then explain how this information can help scientists today.

Why Scientists Study Fossils	What These Studies Tell Us	How These Studies Help Us Today

From the sideline: In your answer, be sure you
- *choose one reason why scientists study fossils;*
- *tell what the text says this tells us; and*
- *explain how this information can help scientists today.*

*Strategies you used:*_____

2. Using details from "Fossils and Earth's History," explain why finding fossils can be exciting.

From the sideline:
- *What is the question asking? Underline key phrases that focus in on what you should include in your answer.*

_____

_____

_____

_____

_____

> *From the sideline: Be sure your answer*
> ■ *tells why finding fossils can be exciting, and*
> ■ *gives details from the story to support your reasons.*

CLEANING UP THE WORLD

© David P. Lewis

My name is Martina. I live in Montauk on Long Island in New York State. I am an environmental scientist.

I first became interested in the environment when my fifth-grade class went out to pick up trash on Earth Day. I couldn't believe how much trash people were just throwing away with no thought at all of what it was doing to the environment for everyone else! Eventually, I went to college to study earth science. I was also interested in ocean life, so I took several courses on oceanography. As part of my school work I had the chance to submerge down to the seafloor in a submarine. You won't believe what I saw one whole mile below the surface of the water! Trash! This really made me determined to do something about the way humans were polluting the environment.

Now the work I do helps the environment. On my job, I study the movement of seawater and how materials such as oil are transported across oceans. We have to be sure that ships that transport oil across the oceans are well maintained and do not leak harmful fuel oils into the water. This could kill sea animals and poison the fish people eat. I also research how pollutants from industries affect water quality. We have to know if industries are dumping harmful chemicals into our waterways.

I search out and fix pollution and other environmental problems. I am proud of what I can accomplish on my job. I test water to make sure it is safe and give advice on how to clean the environment. My co-workers and I have designed safe ways to take harmful chemicals from industries out of our water.

On my job, I get to go out into the field. This might be confusing, but on my job when I say I'm going "into the field" to work it means I'm really going out on the ocean. Fieldwork is work we do outside of the office or laboratory. It is our field laboratory in the outside world. My field laboratory is the ocean because that is the environment where I work most often.

There is other work environmental scientists do, too. We are interested in a good variety of topics. Some of us mix what we know about the environment with biology and focus on protecting animals and plants. Others help to make laws about protecting the environment and help companies follow these laws. Many environmental scientists work in laboratories and offices, and, like me, many do fieldwork.

I am very proud of the work I do. I want the world to be safe for people and animals for a long, long time. We must protect our environment now from harmful pollutants that endanger our water and food. We can't do it alone, though. More people interested in being environmental scientists are needed.

Strategies you used for comprehending and reading critically: _____

_____

_____

3. Using information from "Cleaning Up the World," compare the various jobs environmental scientists do to protect the earth. Use details from the article to support your answer.

_____

_____

_____

_____

_____

> *From the sideline: Be sure your answer*
> ▪ *compares several jobs described in the article and*
> ▪ *uses details from the article to support the comparison.*

*Strategies you used:*_____

THE EXTENDED-RESPONSE QUESTION

Planning Page

Use page 106 to PLAN your writing for question 4. Do NOT write your final answer here. Anything you write on the planning page will NOT count toward your final score. Write your FINAL answer on the lines that follow the question.

From the sideline: Your planning page could consist of
- *a graphic organizer to illustrate the organization of your essay (see the Online Resources section of Chapter 4 for ideas);*
- *an outline; or*
- *well-organized notes sequencing several paragraphs and bulleting details within each paragraph.*

From the sideline: Check.
- *Does your plan focus on answering the question? Reread the question to be sure. If so, continue. If not, go back and revise to refocus.*
- *Does your plan express your judgment or opinion based on details from the passage?*

4. If you were a scientist, would you rather work with fossils or with the environment? Write an essay in which you explain your choice. Use details from "Fossils and Earth's History" and "Cleaning Up the World" to support your explanation.

In your response,

- describe which kind of scientist you'd be,

- explain why, and

- use details from both articles to support your answer.

From the sideline: Also be sure to
- *organize your essay into paragraphs (example: introduction, body, and conclusion) and*
- *check your writing for correct spelling, punctuation, and grammar.*

_____

_____

_____

_____

_____

_____

_____

_____

> *From the sideline: Check.*
> ■ *Are you still focused on answering the question? If so, continue. If not, go back and revise to refocus.*

_____

_____

_____

_____

_____

_____

_____

_____

> *From the sideline: Be sure your essay answers the question. Does it*
> ■ *describe which kind of scientist you'd be,*
> ■ *explain why, and*
> ■ *use details from both articles to support your answer?*
>
> *Have you checked your spelling, punctuation, paragraphing, capitalization, grammar, and language use? (The answer to the extended-response question in Book 3 is used as part of your writing mechanics score.)*

Strategies you used: _____

_____

SCORING

Now, let's look at how your responses will be scored in Book 3. After you read through this section, go back and improve your responses before you check the sample answers at the end of this chapter.

Your responses will be scored in five areas: meaning, development, organization, language use, and conventions (writing mechanics). See Appendix C for two sample scoring rubrics. Use the Grade 6 English Language Arts Rubric Chart to score the four responses in Book 3 for meaning, development, organization, and language use—the first four areas. Each question is not scored separately but as a cluster or group. You will get from 0 to 5 points on the cluster of questions as a whole. The fifth area, conventions, is scored using the Writing Mechanics Rubric Chart, which is also found in Appendix C. On the test, the extended responses in Books 2 and 3 are scored together. You can get 0 to 3 points for conventions.

Now that you know how the scoring works, let's take a look at what each area on the rubrics includes.

1. Meaning: Does your answer show you understand the story and how to answer the questions? To get the top score, you should
   a. answer the questions completely,
   b. show you understand and can interpret the ideas and the topic or theme of the story, and
   c. connect the story to other things you know.
2. Development: Is your answer strong? To get the top score, you should
   a. express your ideas thoroughly and elaborate with details and
   b. pull relevant examples from the story to show you completely understand.

3. Organization: Is your writing structured and easy to follow? To get the top score, you should
   a. be focused and stick to the point and the plan to express your thoughts,
   b. sequence your ideas so they make sense, and
   c. use transitions between paragraphs and ideas.
4. Language use: Is your language interesting and intelligent? To get the top score, you should
   a. write in a way that flows easily, engages the reader, and rouses interest;
   b. use interesting vocabulary such as vivid adjectives and descriptive adverbs that show a high level of vocabulary knowledge and use; and
   c. vary the way you structure your sentences.
5. Conventions: How are your grammar, punctuation, and spelling? To get the top score, you should
   a. proofread very carefully so you have very few, if any, errors;
   b. check all grammar, capitalization, punctuation, and sentence structure;
   c. separate your essay into paragraphs appropriately; and
   d. especially check conventions in your answer to the extended-response question because this is the response that is used as part of your writing mechanics score. See Appendix C for the Writing Mechanics Rubric Chart.

After reading the Scoring section, go back to the guided practice questions in this book and see what you can do to improve your answers and your writing. Then look at the possible responses that are given next. Would you give yourself the top score for this cluster of four questions? Would you give yourself the top score for conventions on the extended response? If not, why not? Which parts of the Scoring section could you improve on even more when you get to the two practice tests in Chapters 6 and 7?

POSSIBLE RESPONSES TO THE SAMPLE QUESTIONS IN THIS CHAPTER

Short-Response Questions

Question 1. The authors of "Fossils and Earth's History" describe several different things fossils tell us about the earth's history. Complete the chart below by identifying one reason scientists study fossils and what they do with the information they obtain. Then explain how this information can help scientists today.

Possible Response

Why Scientists Study Fossils	What These Studies Tell Us	How These Studies Help Us Today
To see what animals and plants were like millions of years ago	*How animals and plants gradually changed*	*Animals and plants might change in the future; fossils can give us ideas how they'll change to adapt to the climate and environment*

Question 2. Using details from "Fossils and Earth's History," explain why finding fossils can be exciting.

Possible Response

Finding fossils can be very exciting. It can be like looking for buried treasure because you may be the very first person to ever see the fossil you find. It can be exciting, too, because you can learn a lot about how the giant landmasses broke apart and how the continents were once connected. The earth, animals, and plants have changed over time. Fossils can teach you what life was like millions of years ago. That's pretty exciting, especially if you like history.

Question 3. Using information from "Cleaning Up the World," compare and contrast the various jobs environmental scientists do to protect the earth. Use details from the article to support your answer.

Possible Response

There are various jobs environmental scientists do to protect the earth. In the article, Martina describes her job, which is to protect the waterways and lives of ocean animals by studying water movement and the transportation of oil across the oceans. She also finds ways to remove pollution from industries out of water. Some environmental scientists work right in the field, but others work in laboratories and offices, like those who protect the earth by making and enforcing laws.

EXTENDED-RESPONSE QUESTION

Question 4. If you were a scientist, would you rather work with fossils or with the environment? Write an essay in which you explain your choice. Use details from "Fossils and Earth's History" and "Cleaning Up the World" to support your explanation.

In your response,

- *describe which kind of scientist you'd be,*
- *explain why, and*
- *use details from both articles to support your answer.*

First, you will plan your essay. You are given a blank space to do this. Here are two examples of how you might quickly organize your essay. In this outline, the main items (I, II, and III) would each be a separate paragraph. The letters under each numeral would include your supporting details from the story.

Outline style:

    I. Introduction
        A. two kinds
        B. prefer env sci
    II. Reasons why
        A. what trash and pollution do
        B. make and enforce laws
        C. fieldwork: digs vs. ocean
        D. my personal experience
    III. Conclusion
        A. both jobs needed
        B. help right away

Graphic style:

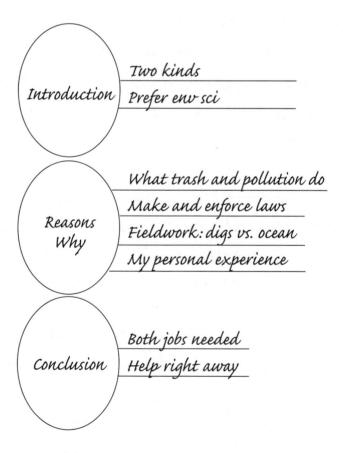

Now, we are ready to look at an example of how this planning helped create a solid, organized essay.

Possible Response

The two articles describe two different types of scientists. In "Fossils and Earth's History," we learn about scientists who work with fossils. They study fossils to learn about what animals and plants looked like and how they acted millions of years ago. The article also says that the coal we burn for heat is made of fossils. People need fuel, so this part of studying fossils is very important. "Cleaning Up the World" describes scientists who work with the environment to protect the earth, people, and animals. Both types of scientists are needed in our world, and their jobs are very important. If I had a choice, though, I would prefer to be an environmental scientist who could help keep the world safe from pollution.

There are a few reasons why I would prefer to be an environmental scientist. First, like Martina, I think it is important to keep our waterways safe. We get food from the oceans. If the water is polluted, the fish will be poisoned and dangerous to eat. Environmental scientists keep track of ships transporting oil, which can be very harmful to fish, across the oceans. If these ships leaked oil into the oceans, it could affect sea life and humans. Next, I think it is important to make and enforce laws so people will take care of the environment. If we have more scientists making laws, people will have to pay attention to them. Finally, I would prefer to be out on the ocean working instead of digging up sand and rocks to find fossils. I think digging would be boring, but the sea would be exciting. I have spent time vacationing at the seashore, and I really enjoy the sea air and being out on the water.

While both types of scientists are very necessary and important, I would prefer the job of the environmental scientist. There are a variety of things these scientists can study. It is important for people to pay attention to our environment right away.

ONLINE RESOURCES

Here are some great web sites for learning more about graphic organizers:

■ *http://www.edhelperclipart.com/clipart/teachers/ org-howtouse.pdf*
■ *http://www.edhelper.com/teachers/Sorting_graphic_ organizers.htm*
■ *http://www.edhelper.com/teachers/Sequencing_graphic_ organizers.htm*

CONGRATULATIONS!

Now you know what Book 3 is all about. You have read about the parts of the test, the test directions, and the question breakdown. You have also learned a number of strategies for

■ reading critically and
■ planning and writing critical essays

while you practiced sample questions from the test.

Next, you should continue on to Chapters 6 and 7. There you will find two complete practice tests to help you apply what you have learned. All the answers are provided, too, with explanations. After taking these practice tests, check the multiple-choice answers in Book 1 against the answers at the end of each chapter. Score your short and extended responses in Books 2 and 3 using the two rubrics in Appendix C. You also may want to ask a friend, family member, or teacher to score your responses in Books 2 and 3. Ask them what you could do to improve your writing and your scores. Good luck!

Chapter 6

PRACTICE TEST 1

Tips:

To do your best

- carefully read all the directions;
- plan how you will use your time wisely;
- read each question thoroughly; and
- before choosing your response, think about the answer.

BOOK 1: READING

26 Multiple-Choice Questions

55 Minutes to Complete—Work Until You Come to STOP

Each Correct Response Is Worth 1 Point

DIRECTIONS

In Book 1, you will read four or five passages and answer a few questions about each one. Fill in the answers to Book 1 on the bubble sheet on the next page by filling in the letter that matches your answer. Do not write your answers on the test pages. You may make notes or marks on the test pages as you read, though. Be sure to answer all the questions. The correct answers, with explanations, can be found at the end of this chapter.

BOOK 1—ANSWER SHEET

1. Ⓐ Ⓑ Ⓒ Ⓓ

2. Ⓐ Ⓑ Ⓒ Ⓓ

3. Ⓐ Ⓑ Ⓒ Ⓓ

4. Ⓐ Ⓑ Ⓒ Ⓓ

5. Ⓐ Ⓑ Ⓒ Ⓓ

6. Ⓐ Ⓑ Ⓒ Ⓓ

7. Ⓐ Ⓑ Ⓒ Ⓓ

8. Ⓐ Ⓑ Ⓒ Ⓓ

9. Ⓐ Ⓑ Ⓒ Ⓓ

10. Ⓐ Ⓑ Ⓒ Ⓓ

11. Ⓐ Ⓑ Ⓒ Ⓓ

12. Ⓐ Ⓑ Ⓒ Ⓓ

13. Ⓐ Ⓑ Ⓒ Ⓓ

14. Ⓐ Ⓑ Ⓒ Ⓓ

15. Ⓐ Ⓑ Ⓒ Ⓓ

16. Ⓐ Ⓑ Ⓒ Ⓓ

17. Ⓐ Ⓑ Ⓒ Ⓓ

18. Ⓐ Ⓑ Ⓒ Ⓓ

19. Ⓐ Ⓑ Ⓒ Ⓓ

20. Ⓐ Ⓑ Ⓒ Ⓓ

21. Ⓐ Ⓑ Ⓒ Ⓓ

22. Ⓐ Ⓑ Ⓒ Ⓓ

23. Ⓐ Ⓑ Ⓒ Ⓓ

24. Ⓐ Ⓑ Ⓒ Ⓓ

25. Ⓐ Ⓑ Ⓒ Ⓓ

26. Ⓐ Ⓑ Ⓒ Ⓓ

Directions: Read this poem, called "Autumn's Last Dance," about a charcoal-colored cat. Then answer questions 1 through 5.

AUTUMN'S LAST DANCE

Julia Baxter-MacGregor

1 The charcoal cat purrs sleepily on the windowsill,
    Staring out at the darkening sky.
    Clouds float by that look like her.
    She watches them go by.

5 The wind lifts leaves from their resting places,
    And takes them to places far away.
    She sees them dance around the sky,
    And likes to watch them play.

9 Now suddenly a new dancer appears,
    To take part in the celebration.
    It flies as lightly as a butterfly,
    Above fall's creation.

13 The cat raises her head and stares outside
    At this new addition to the scene.
    She watches as it fills the air,
    And covers any green.

17   It is new, yet familiar, dancing around the trees,

Swirling and floating, then falling softly to the ground.

It speaks of the end of autumn,

Without even making a sound.

21   The charcoal cat sits on the windowsill, grooming her fur.

She takes one more look out the window, before deciding to go.

It is time to take a trip outside,

To visit the season's first snow.

© Elena Elisseeva

1. What is the main theme of "Autumn's Last Dance"?

  A. The charcoal cat is self-indulgent and lazy.

  B. The seasons are changing.

  C. The leaves are like dancers.

  D. The cat is enjoying the day.

2. Read lines 5 through 8 from the poem.

> The wind lifts leaves from their resting places,
> And takes them to places far away.
> She sees them dance around the sky,
> And likes to watch them play.

According to the poem, which of these phrases **best** characterizes the leaves?

A. tired

B. scared and nervous

C. sad

D. playful and happy

3. What is the pattern of each stanza of this poem?

A. The second and fourth lines rhyme.

B. None of the lines rhyme.

C. Each pair of lines rhyme.

D. All the lines rhyme within each stanza.

4. The two dancers in this poem are

A. the cat and the trees.

B. the cat and the leaves.

C. the leaves and the clouds.

D. the leaves and the snow.

5. In which stanza does the author first introduce the snow?

A. Stanza 2

B. Stanza 3

C. Stanza 4

D. Stanza 6

Go On

Directions: Read this ancient tale. Then answer questions 6 through 11.

HOW THE FOOLISH OLD MAN MOVED MOUNTAINS: AN ANCIENT CHINESE TALE

Retold by Ying Tang

© Matt Apps

Yugong was a ninety-year-old man who lived in a small village located at the north of two high mountains, Mount Taishing and Mount Wangwu.

Stretching over a wide expanse of land, the mountains blocked Yugong's way making it inconvenient for him, his family, and other villagers to get to the town on the south side of the mountains. One day Yugong decided to call a family meeting and announced, "I think we should level these two mountains and pave a road to the next village. What do you think?"

All but his wife agreed with him. "Honey, you are just an old man. How on earth do you think you can level Mount Taishing and Mount Wangwu? What do you think you can accomplish?"

Yugong declared with confidence, "I know I am not getting young, and *I* may not live to see the new road. But, we have children and grandchildren. They can help me. If they can't do it in their lifetime, there will be great-grandchildren to follow in their footsteps. The mountains don't grow any taller, so eventually we will be able to finish the task."

So Yugong, his children, and his grandchildren started to break up rocks and remove the soil.

On the bank of the Yellow River dwelled an old man much respected for his wisdom. When he saw the back-breaking labor of Yugong's family, he ridiculed Yugong saying, "Aren't you foolish, my friend? You are very old now, and with whatever remains of your waning strength, you won't be able to remove even a corner of the mountain."

The other villagers also laughed at the idea of leveling the mountains. They called Yugong "The Old Fool" and made fun of him and his idea.

Summer went by and winter came. Yugong and his family continued with the task, despite the villagers' ridicule and criticism.

When the guardian gods of the mountains saw how determined Yugong and his crew were, the gods were struck with fear. They reported the incident to the Emperor of Heavens.

Filled with admiration for Yugong, the Emperor of Heavens eventually ordered two mighty gods to carry the mountains away. From then on, there were no mountains blocking the way from Yugong's village to the other village.

6. Read this quote from the story.

   > "Aren't you foolish, my friend? You are very old now, and with whatever remains of your waning strength, you won't be able to remove even a corner of the mountain."

   In the second sentence, the word *waning* means

   A. fading.

   B. increasing.

   C. bulky.

   D. swelling.

7. Which of the following details from the story explains why the old man thought the task was possible?

   A. He thought the gods would be struck with fear.

   B. The villagers ridiculed and criticized Yugong.

   C. They needed a road to the next town.

   D. The mountains don't grow any taller, so he knew eventually they would be able to finish the task.

8. Which of these topics would **best** fit as a logical part of this story?

   A. Why the family and other townspeople wanted to get to the town on the other side of the mountains.

   B. The economy of the area today.

   C. The cost of moving the mountains.

   D. Names of mountains in China today.

9. What is the **most likely** reason why Yugong wanted to level the mountains?

   A. He thought it would be a healthful way to spend his last days on earth.

   B. He was a man who liked a challenge.

   C. He knew his family and others would benefit by getting to the next village more easily.

   D. He thought it would keep his children and grandchildren from fighting with each other.

10. What message was Yugong **most likely** trying to get across to his children and grandchildren by leveling the mountain?

   A. No task is impossible if we work together with a common goal.

   B. The villagers are unwise, but our family is very wise.

   C. The gods will help us when we need them.

   D. Hard labor is honest work.

11. Why did the Emperor of the Heavens have the mountains moved?

   A. The mountains were needed elsewhere.

   B. The mountains were blocking the rain.

   C. He wanted the two villages to join and work together.

   D. He was impressed by Yugong's family's determination.

Go On

Directions: Read this article about fall leaves. Then answer questions 12 through 16.

WHY FALL IS SO COLORFUL

Julia Baxter-MacGregor

Fall is a beautiful time of year in many places around the United States. The weather becomes cooler, and the once green leaves on our trees turn beautiful shades of yellow, orange, and red. While we all enjoy the colors of autumn, did you ever wonder what happens to make the green leaves of summer become the brightly colored leaves of fall? To understand this, we need first understand what jobs leaves have in nature.

Leaves are like food factories in nature. Trees and other plants take in water from the ground through their roots. Then they take a gas called carbon dioxide from the air. The plants use the energy from the sun (sunlight) to turn the water and the carbon dioxide into glucose. Glucose is a kind of sugar that plants use for food, very much like we use sugar to give us energy. Plants use this food to grow. The name for this process is photosynthesis, which means "putting together with light." Chlorophyll is a chemical that helps make this happen and that makes plants and leaves green.

During the summer days when there is lots of sunlight, leaves make more glucose than the tree needs for its energy and growth. As autumn gets closer, and the days get shorter, there is less daylight. When there is less sunlight, plants begin to shut down their food production. You might look at it this way: when you are on summer vacation, resting from a hard year at school, trees are working very hard to make and store their food. When you go back to school in the fall, trees and plants begin to get ready to "go on vacation" over the winter to take a break from all of the photosynthesizing they did over the summer. When hardworking trees begin to take this rest, leaves begin to change color. This is a signal to us that trees are planning to take their long winter vacation to rest for next spring and summer's food production.

When sunlight decreases, trees make less and less chlorophyll. Over this time period, the tree eventually stops making it all together. When that happens, the green begins to fade, and the other colors that were also in the leaves begin to show through. Yes, orange, yellow, brown, and red are colors that were in the leaves all along. However, they were covered up by the green chlorophyll. It's as if you were wearing a green coat over a brightly colored outfit and you finally take your coat off!

The type of tree affects the colors the leaves will change. The leaves of oak trees can turn brown or red, while maple trees can become brilliant orange-red, and birch trees can turn yellow. The weather also affects how brilliant the color will be. The brightest colors occur when there is a warm, wet spring, a summer that isn't too hot or too dry, and a fall with lots of warm sunny days and cool but not freezing nights. If it freezes too soon, the frost will kill the leaves, turning them brown and making them drop too early.

So, next time you are walking to school or around your house crunching the beautiful orange, red, brown, and yellow leaves under your feet, remember that the trees above are getting ready for their winter vacation. The trees don't die; they just take a break from their work, just like we do! But don't worry, they will come back from this vacation in the spring, ready to go to work to produce new green leaves for us to enjoy on our summer vacation.

12. Why are leaves like food factories in nature?

   A. Trees make sap that can be made into maple syrup.

   B. Leaves use resources from the ground, air, and sun to make food for the tree.

   C. People can eat the fruit many trees produce for food.

   D. They produce chlorophyll.

13. According to the article, what is the **main reason** why fall is so colorful?

   A. Maple trees turn brilliant orange-red.

   B. Trees make their food in the winter.

   C. Leaves make less chlorophyll than they do in the summer.

   D. Fall is an active time of year for trees as they produce glucose.

14. According to the article, how do trees "go on vacation"?

   A. They produce new green leaves.

   B. They produce more chlorophyll.

   C. They take a break from photosynthesizing.

   D. They begin to produce food.

15. The author describes chlorophyll by writing:

It's as if you were wearing a green coat over a brightly colored outfit and you finally take your coat off!

Why does the author **most likely** describe it this way?

A. to help you picture how chlorophyll works

B. to explain how freezing temperatures affect photo-synthesis

C. to show how trees produce new green leaves

D. to describe how trees die

16. "Why Fall Is So Colorful" is an essay that is most like a

A. folktale.

B. fairy tale.

C. report.

D. journal.

Go On

Directions: Read the following story about the USS *Slater*, which was a Naval Destroyer Escort warship during World War II. Answer Questions 17 through 22.

---

moored—docked

convoy—a group of ships that travel together

THE USS SLATER

Courtesy of the Destroyer Escort Historical Museum

During World War II, 563 Destroyer Escorts battled Nazi U-Boats on the North Atlantic Ocean. They protected convoys of men and material. In the Pacific Ocean, they stood in line to defend naval task forces from Japanese submarines and air attacks.

© zmajdoo

Today, only one of these ships remains afloat in the United States. It is the USS *Slater*. Moored on the Hudson River in Albany, New York, the USS *Slater* has undergone an extensive ten-year restoration that has returned the ship to her former glory. The ship is open to the public from April through November with hour-long guided tours and youth group overnight camping. Visitors learn about the sacrifices involved in life aboard a World War II Destroyer Escort. The ship has also become a popular destination for naval reunion groups.

When you step aboard the USS *Slater*, you are actually stepping back in time. The USS *Slater* was not designed as a tourist attraction. It is a warship.

Restoration

Professionals donate their time to bring about the ship's transformation by repairing and restoring the ship to its original shape. For example, the electrical team worked for months in the dark in freezing temperatures with only flashlights to guide them in order to restore electrical power to the ship. Engineers meet on Saturdays to work on the ship's diesel engine.

Maintenance crews gather to chip paint, paint, clean, and remove layers of tile to restore the ship's spaces. Tour guides, many of them Navy veterans, lead visitors through the ship to help them gain a sense of how the 216-man crew functioned. Others actively promote the ship and seek funding to fuel the restoration. The collections team catalogs the hundreds of photos, documents, and personal papers donated to the museum.

Name

The Destroyer Escorts were named for Naval heroes, particularly those from early in World War II. The USS *Slater* is named for Frank O. Slater of Alabama, a sailor killed aboard the USS *San Francisco* during the Battle of Guadalcanal in 1942. During the battle, Slater refused to abandon his gun in the face of an onrushing Japanese torpedo plane. With cool determination and utter disregard for his own personal safety, he kept blazing away until the hostile craft plunged out of the sky in a flaming dive and crashed on his station. He gallantly gave up his life in the defense of his country.

17. The author **most likely** uses two subheadings within the article in order to

   A. organize the article's content.

   B. show the cause and effect of the restoration and naming.

   C. compare how the ship was restored with how it was named.

   D. confuse the reader.

18. According to the article, what can a visitor touring the USS *Slater* expect to find on board the USS *Slater*?

   A. a plaque about Frank O. Slater

   B. electrical power

   C. a gift shop

   D. a restaurant

19. What is the **main purpose** of this article?

    A. to inform readers about the USS *Slater*

    B. to persuade people to help restore the USS *Slater*

    C. to compare the USS *Slater* with other historical museums

    D. to show the effects of the USS *Slater*'s restoration

20. From this article, what do we **definitely** know about the USS *Slater* today?

    A. It was attacked by enemy forces during World War II.

    B. It is the most popular historical museum in New York State.

    C. It is a historical museum that is toured by visitors.

    D. It costs $8 for an adult to tour the museum.

21. According to the article, how does Frank O. Slater's death compare with what the USS *Slater* did during World War II?

    A. Both fought in the Battle of Guadalcanal.

    B. Both gallantly protected others.

    C. Both were involved in World War I.

    D. Only the USS *Slater* was involved in World War II.

22. What does the word *restoration* mean in this article?

    A. to have a good reputation

    B. to use the ship as storage for World War II documents

    C. to repair to the original shape or condition

    D. to train new naval officers

Go On

Directions: **Read this story about Niagara Falls before answering questions 23 through 26.**

© Willem Dijkstra

What do you think of when you hear the words *Niagara Falls*? Most likely, you think of waterfalls. Maybe you've heard stories of people trying to ride over the falls in a barrel. Or maybe you know a couple who was married or had their honeymoon in the city of Niagara Falls.

Last summer, my family and I went to Niagara Falls. I wanted to remember my trip and what we did every day so I brought my notebook. Every night I took a few minutes to write about what we did that day. Here is what I wrote.

July 2, 2007

Today we flew from the Albany Airport to Buffalo, New York. It was a pretty short flight. I was hoping to see the Falls from the airplane, but we didn't. When we landed, we rented a car and drove to the New York side of Niagara Falls. You can see the falls from the New York side, or you can cross the border and go into Canada. We are staying in a hotel on the New York side. Our room has a view of the river, and it has a whirlpool tub. When we go outside our hotel room, you can actually hear the waterfalls. I can't wait until we go see them tomorrow morning. Tonight we're going to have dinner and drive around town a little. Then we're going to make it an early night so we can get up early. I can't wait until tomorrow!

July 3, 2007

We saw the falls today. It was spectacular. First, when we got up, there was a continental breakfast downstairs in the hotel's restaurant. There were danishes, donuts, juices, milk, and coffee. Then, we excitedly drove to the American Falls. I never thought it would be so BIG or so LOUD!!! We were holding our hands up to our ears because the noise of the falls was so loud. It was just water falling over rocks, but it made a loud rumbling noise like continuous thunder. Gradually, we got used to the noise, though. Next, we drove over to the Horseshoe Canadian Falls. There was a park, more restaurants, and a big gift shop. We mostly spent our day walking around and staring at the falls from every different angle. We took a tour of the falls where the guide takes you through this tunnel. You end up behind the falls. There was a big window you could look through to see that you were really behind the falls as they fell over the crest.

July 4, 2007

This was our last day to spend time at the falls. We got up early again and drove to the falls. We took a tour on the *Maid of the Mist*, which is a boat tour that brings you right up to the bottom of the falls. I was surprised to learn that The *Maid of the Mist* has operated since 1846, and famous people like past presidents Theodore Roosevelt and Jimmy Carter and Princess Diana of Wales have taken the *Maid of the Mist* boat tours. The ponchos they give you do keep out most of the water, but the mist from the water feels like someone is squirting you with a squirt bottle. If we thought the falls were loud before, they were even louder from the boat.

We also visited the New York State Observation Tower platform. It is 200 feet above the base of the Niagara Gorge, and you can see the falls really well. To end the day, we saw fireworks over the falls from the New York side. This was the perfect way to end our special Fourth of July weekend.

July 5, 2007

This morning we flew back in to Albany Airport. I'm really tired. Today I just rested on the couch and read. It was a really great trip. I'd like to go back some day, but first I have to rest my eardrums!

23. What would be the **best** title for this passage?

   A. "My Family"

   B. "My Family's Fourth of July Vacation"

   C. "The *Maid of the Mist*"

   D. "Flying to Niagara Falls"

24. What does this article **most closely** resemble?

   A. a journal

   B. a tall tale

   C. a newspaper article

   D. an autobiography

25. What is the overall structure of this article?

   A. cause and effect

   B. time sequence

   C. compare and contrast

   D. problem followed by solution

26. According to the passage, which of the following sentences is an opinion?

   A. Jimmy Carter rode the *Maid of the Mist* boat tour.

   B. Albany Airport has a flight to Buffalo, New York.

   C. The falls are unbearably loud.

   D. You can see the falls from the Canadian or the New York side.

STOP

BOOK 2: LISTENING AND WRITING

3 Short Responses and 1 Extended Response

60 Minutes to Complete *After* Passage Is Read Twice

Book 2 Responses Are Worth a Total of 5 Points

DIRECTIONS

Book 2 asks you to write about a passage that will be read to you. When you write your responses, DO NOT write about your personal opinions. However, you should make connections beyond the reading in the final essay response (question 30). Before you begin this part of the practice test, it is recommended that you review the scoring rubric in Appendix C to guide your writing. Your responses will be scored based on the following:

- Have you clearly organized your ideas?
- Have you clearly expressed your ideas?
- Have you completely and accurately answered the questions?
- Have you supported the ideas in your responses by examples from the passage?
- Is your writing enjoyable and interesting to the reader?
- Have you used accurate grammar, spelling, punctuation, and paragraphing?

In Book 2 in this practice test, you will listen to a story called "What Has Value." Then, you will read the questions in this part of the test and write your answers to show you understood the story.

The story will be read to you not once, but twice. Listen carefully and take notes on the story. Use your notes to answer the following questions about the story.

When you have completed your answers, use the rubric in Appendix C to score your responses. Then, read the sample responses at the end of this chapter and use this model and the rubric to revise and improve your responses and score.

Note to Reader: Read the entire passage two times from beginning to end. Start with the title and author each time. Read at a comfortable pace.

WHAT HAS VALUE

Elaine Lawrence

A long time ago my kid sister, Charlene, used to irritate me to no end. Make no mistake, she was an annoying little kid. She is six years younger than me, but that didn't stop her from always wanting to do everything that I was doing and becoming involved in everything that I was doing. I often scolded her—sometimes I would yell at her—to stop sticking her nose into my business. But do you think she ever listened to me?

Ever since I can remember, I've always been a collector of toy train sets. They were very valuable because they were worth a lot of money. I was very protective of them and kept Charlene far away from them so she wouldn't break anything. When I was twelve my dad built a large shed out in back of our house in Tennessee. We had the understanding that this shed would be a kind of playhouse, maybe for him as well as for me. He often helped me build long plywood tables so we could assemble whole miniature towns out of train tracks, tiny toy people figures, models of buildings and traffic lights and roads, and, of course, various types of trains. I guess you could say my father spoiled me back in those days. I had many different types of train sets, antiques as well as new. Each and every train set ran on electricity, and some made quite realistic noises when they went whistling around the tracks. One time, when we got four sets of trains going at once, I closed my eyes. It sounded to me as if we were actually at a real railway station.

You might be wondering what the trains have to do with my sister. One day when I was thirteen, my little sister snuck into the train shed to play with the equipment on her own. I was outside cleaning my bicycle when my father came out.

"Dinner's almost ready. Where's your sister? I thought she was with you," he said.

Just then we heard a loud crash from the shed. We heard Charlene—screaming! My dad and I ran into the shed and found Charlene on the floor. One of my train set tables had landed on the upper part of her body. My father lifted the heavy table as if it weighed nothing, and he threw it aside.

My precious trains smashed into the wall, but I didn't even care. All I could think about was how my sister was. I could see her face had some blood on it. My father started crying—like I'd never seen him cry before. I could tell he wanted to pick her up, to embrace her, but he was torn. He knew he shouldn't move her. Doing so could cause her to become even more badly injured. I yelled to him that I was going back to the house to call 911. My mother, never taking her eyes off of Charlene, rode with Charlene in the ambulance as it sped away to the hospital.

I had never been that scared in all my life. All kinds of thoughts went racing through my head. I realized how much I greatly loved my sister. I also thought about how often I had been very mean to her. I was filled with deep, sad regrets. I told myself I would never ignore her or shoo her away from me again. I would give her all the attention she would ever want from me.

My sister gradually recovered. We have been very close ever since that tragic day when I learned what has real value. We fixed up the trains again, and now you can find my dad, me, and Charlene out in the backyard shed every weekend working on some sort of hobby. I couldn't imagine my life without my sister. You can replace materials things, like trains, but you can't replace your relationship with a family member or someone you love. That has real value.

NOTES

NOTES

STOP

Start Timing the 60 Minutes
After the Passage Has Been Read Twice.

27. Complete the chart that follows by describing what the author valued and why. Use details from the story to support your answer.

What the Author Valued	Why She Valued It

28. How does the author let the reader know that the characters in the story were very upset by the accident?

_____

_____

_____

_____

_____

_____

_____

_____

29. Why is the title "What Has Value" appropriate for the story? Support your explanation with details and information from the story.

_____

_____

_____

_____

_____

_____

_____

_____

Go On

PLANNING PAGE

PLAN your writing for question 30 on this page. DO NOT write your final essay here, however. Whatever you write on this page WILL NOT be scored as your final response. Write your final essay response on the lines on the next pages.

30. The author Elaine's feelings about her sister Charlene change from the beginning to the end of the passage. Write an essay to describe what Elaine's feelings were toward Charlene at the beginning. Then tell how and why they changed. Use information from the passage to support your response.

In your response, make sure that you

■ describe Elaine's feelings toward Charlene at the beginning of the story;

■ describe why Elaine felt as she did at the beginning;

■ describe what happened to change Elaine's feelings toward Charlene;

■ explain why Elaine's feelings change;

■ include information and details from the passage to support your response; and

■ check your grammar, spelling, and punctuation.

_____

_____

_____

_____

_____

_____

_____

_____

_____

Go On

_____

_____

_____

_____

_____

_____

_____

_____

_____

_____

_____

_____

_____

_____

_____

STOP

BOOK 3: READING AND WRITING

3 Short Responses and 1 Extended Response

60 Minutes

Book 3 Responses Are Worth a Total of 5 Points

DIRECTIONS

Book 3 asks you to write about two passages that you read. When you write your responses, DO NOT write about your personal opinions. Your responses will be scored based on the following:

- Have you clearly organized your ideas?
- Have you clearly expressed your ideas?
- Have you completely and accurately answered the questions?
- Have you supported the ideas in your responses by examples from the passage?
- Is your writing enjoyable and interesting to the reader?
- Have you used accurate grammar, spelling, punctuation, and paragraphing?

In Book 3 in this practice test, you will read two passages. One is called "Say 'Cheese'" and is about photography as a hobby. The other passage is called "Music Soothes the Savage Beast" and is about music as a hobby. Use what you read in the passages to answer questions 31 through 34. You may look back and reread the passages any time you want to while answering the questions. Sample responses can be found at the end of this chapter.

> **portfolio**—an organized collection of a person's work

SAY "CHEESE"

I'm not someone who likes to have my picture taken. I don't feel comfortable in front of a camera. I was never good at smiling pretty and saying "Cheese"! I'm just too self-conscious. But I love being the one behind the camera taking pictures. There is something creative and wonderful about being a photographer.

When I was ten years old, my aunt gave me my first real camera. It wasn't just a disposable or throw-away camera that you get for $5 at the local department store. It was a digital camera with a zoom-in lens and lots of different settings to control the lighting and to focus. The nice thing about it was that because it was a digital camera, I could take as many pictures as I wanted to and then just delete the ones I didn't like. I didn't have the expense of having all the pictures developed. It gave me a chance to practice and get better at choosing which angle to shoot from and other methods that I learned to improve my pictures.

I love to take photos of everything—people, scenery, animals. Sometimes I'm surprised how my pictures turn out. It isn't always the unusual or beautiful things that I photograph that end up being my favorite or best work. My favorite all-time picture is one of a path in the woods behind our farm. I just love the way the light shines down, lighting the path through the tall trees. It looks very majestic and spiritual. Out of about 50 pictures I took in the woods that day, this one really stood out as

© RJR

the best one because it seemed to be saying something to me like "come this way." I think the best pictures talk to us.

My friends say I have a "good eye." That encourages me to try to improve my skills even more. They tell me my photographs look natural, and I seem to know what makes a shot interesting. They say I'm good at capturing the right pose or moment so the photo portrays a message to the person looking at it. I think part of being able to do that comes from practice and part of it is just enjoying what you are doing. When I shoot pictures, I try to capture the feelings people are sharing or the way a scene makes me feel as I look at it. I like the idea that people can relive the feelings they were experiencing anytime they look at my photos.

I want to create a portfolio of the pictures I have taken for a couple of reasons. First, I have so many pictures that I need to organize them as I keep adding to my collection. I enjoy sharing my work with my friends and family, but I need to group them in an appealing way. Taking photographs is a very creative way to express yourself. Organizing my work into a portfolio would help me tell stories through my pictures—not just my stories, but other people's stories, too. I also want to organize a portfolio of my work in hopes that I might be able to sell some of my photography. This can be a very expensive hobby. Not only are cameras expensive, but there are all kinds of attachments and lighting effects you have to purchase if you are serious about taking the best possible pictures you can. Of course, there's the expense of getting your pictures developed, too. As I become more knowledgeable and skilled about photography, my pictures are getting better and better. My neighbor, who is a professional photographer, has been helping me research places that buy photos and hire photographers. I would not only be happy to earn money by selling my photos, but I would also be very proud that someone liked my work enough to actually pay for it!

I know I still have a great deal to learn about taking photographs. But I also know that I really enjoy being a photographer, so I am willing to invest the time and energy it will take to continue to improve. I am looking forward maybe to developing this hobby of mine into a small business some day. There are many different types of jobs for photographers, from people who sell their photos to magazines to those who sell their work in galleries. Who knows! Maybe one day you'll see one of my photos for sale in a shop window or maybe I'll be the photographer at your wedding! If you see me behind a camera, be sure to smile pretty and say "Cheese!"

31. In the chart that follows, identify who influenced the author's interest in photography and how.

Person or People Who Influenced Author	How Person or People Influenced Author

32. Use information from "Say 'Cheese'" to support the opinion that photography makes a good hobby.

_____

_____

_____

_____

_____

_____

Go On

> **cadence**—A series of musical chords that are played together.

MUSIC SOOTHES THE SAVAGE BEAST

Everyone should have a hobby—a special interest that they enjoy doing just for themselves. At the end of a long day, everyone should have a hobby that will help them relax. My hobby is music. Whether I pick up my guitar and start strumming a few chords or I lie on my bed and listen to a CD, I can feel all the worries and stress of the day fall away. All I can think about is the feel of the strings under my fingertips and the melodious, rich sounds of the music. The music soothes and refreshes me. The expression "Music soothes the savage beast" certainly is true in my case.

I like music for many reasons. First, it lets me express my feelings. When I'm energetic I pick loud tunes. I bang out classic rock songs on my guitar and sing loudly with my bedroom door shut. When I'm done, I feel better, like I've downloaded some heavy feelings that I had to get off my chest. I feel stronger then. Music offers so many different kinds of sounds. There's country, jazz, classical music, rap, hip hop; and when you're sad, you can even sing the blues.

I also like music because you can share it with others. It can bring people together. Sometimes I get together with friends who play different instruments and we practice songs together. We teach each other new chords or a new cadence. When I'm with my friends, I'm the one who plays the guitar—the "guitar man." I like being called that because I have a talent no one else in the group does. I add to the group by being the guitar man in a way no one else can. Usually when my family or friends get together, music is always a part of the occasion, whether it's a CD playing in the background, some of us playing our instruments, or people singing or dancing to whatever music fits the occasion.

The only downfall I can see to music is that people have different tastes in music. Some people only like to listen to country music or pop music. They might not tolerate listening to the kind of music other people like. For example, my parents listen to jazz all the time. When I play country music, they usually ask me to close the door or turn the volume down. But that's all right with me, as long as I have my music to sooth the beast in me.

33. The author says, "At the end of a long day, everyone should have a hobby that will help them relax." Describe how what the author does in the evening to relax is similar to what you might do. How is it different from what you might do? Use details and information from the article to support your comparison.

_____

_____

_____

_____

_____

Go On

PLANNING PAGE

PLAN your writing for question 34 on this page. DO NOT write your final essay here, however. Whatever you write on this page WILL NOT be scored as your final response. Write your final essay response on the lines on the next pages.

34. The authors of "Say 'Cheese' " and "Music Soothes the Savage Beast" both have hobbies they enjoy for different reasons. Write an essay in which you explain which hobby you would prefer and why. Use details from both articles to support your response.

In your response, make sure that you

- tell which hobby you would prefer, photography or music;
- explain why you would prefer that hobby over the other;
- include information and details from both passages to support your response; and
- check your grammar, spelling, and punctuation.

_____

_____

_____

_____

_____

_____

_____

_____

_____

Go On

_____

_____

_____

_____

_____

_____

_____

_____

_____

_____

_____

_____

_____

_____

_____

_____

_____

STOP

ANSWERS AND EXPLANATIONS

BOOK 1: READING

"Autumn's Last Dance"

1. **B** The theme of changing seasons runs throughout the poem.

2. **D** The leaves are dancing and playing.

3. **A** The second and fourth lines of each stanza rhyme.

4. **D** The leaves and the snow are described as dancers in the poem.

5. **B** The snow is introduced when the author writes, "Now suddenly a new dancer appears."

"How the Foolish Old Man Moved Mountains"

6. **A** *Waning* means fading or decreasing.

7. **D** The reason the old man gives in the poem is that the mountain won't get taller.

8. **A** This story is set in China a long time ago, so what's going on in China today doesn't connect to this story. Also, it didn't cost any money to move the mountain.

9. **C** This is the only choice supported by evidence in the story.

10. **A** This theme runs throughout the story.

11. **D** We're told in the story that the Emperor of the Heavens admired Yugong.

"Why Fall Is So Colorful"

12. **B** Factories manufacture things. The tree uses resources to make food.

13. **C** Trees make less chlorophyll, so they change colors, making fall colorful.

14. **C** Trees and leaves become less active in the fall and winter according to the article.

15. **A** The author describes the process in a visual way to help the reader understand.

"The USS *Slater*"

16. **C** The article informs the reader like a report.

17. **A** Subheadings help to organize the structure of a passage.

18. **B** The only answer we're told can be found on the ship is electricity because we're told it isn't set up like a tourist attraction. We know electricity was one of the things restored.

19. **A** The article tells us information (informs). It does not persuade, compare, or tell effects.

20. **C** The only fact stated in the story is that the USS *Slater* is a historical museum.

21. **B** This is the only answer supported by details in the story.

22. **C** We're told volunteers and others are working to restore the ship to its original condition.

Story About Niagara Falls

23. **B** This title represents the whole story, while the other choices represent just a detail from part of the story.

24. **A** The dates and retelling of events represent a journal.

25. **B** The dates indicate a time sequence format.

26. **C** The other choices are facts, but it is a matter of opinion whether someone considers the falls unbearably loud.

BOOK 2: LISTENING AND WRITING

"What Has Value"

27. Complete the chart that follows by describing what the author valued and why. Use details from the story to support your answer.

What the Author Valued	Why She Valued It
Her trains	*They were expensive antiques worth a lot of money.*

Another acceptable answer:

Her sister—because she could never replace her relationship with her sister

28. How does the author let the reader know that the characters in the story were very upset by the accident?

Sample Response

The author shows the characters were very upset by the accident by the way she describes how the family reacted. Her father was crying. He wanted to hold her, but he knew he shouldn't move her. Her mother never took her eyes off Charlene in the ambulance. Elaine called 911.

29. Why is the title "What Has Value" appropriate for the story? Support your explanation with details and information from the story.

Sample Response

The main theme of the story is about what the author learns to value. She changes from valuing the trains to valuing her relationship with her sister because of the accident. The title "What Has Value" tells the reader the story is going to be about what the author values.

30. The author Elaine's feelings about her sister Charlene change from the beginning to the end of the passage. Write an essay describing what Elaine's feelings were toward Charlene at the beginning. Then tell how and why they changed. Use information from the passage to support your response.

In your response, make sure that you

■ describe Elaine's feelings toward Charlene at the beginning of the story;

■ describe why Elaine felt as she did at the beginning;

■ describe what happened to change Elaine's feelings toward Charlene;

■ explain why Elaine's feelings change;

■ include information and details from the passage to support your response; and

■ check your grammar, spelling, and punctuation.

Sample Planning Page

While your planning page is not graded, take some time to outline the structure of your essay and to plan which information from the story you will include. You certainly do not have to use a formal outline as demonstrated here, but be sure to plan what you will include in each paragraph. We have used a formal outline structure here to help you visualize the five paragraphs and contents of each in a very clear way.

I. Introduction
    A. valued trains at beginning
    B. valued sister at end after accident
II. Supporting details
    A. beginning
        1. annoying
        2. afraid she'd break trains
        3. wanted to do everything Elaine did
    B. after accident
        1. worried about Charlene
        2. regrets
        3. realized she valued her sister
III. Connections
    A. younger sisters and brothers can be annoying
    B. something we value
IV. Conclusion
    A. how she changed
    B. message of story

Sample Response

"What Has Value" is a story about a girl named Elaine and how she learns what has value in life. At the beginning of the story, Elaine tells about her trains and how protective she was of them. Then, her sister Charlene gets hurt when the train's table falls on her. This accident helps Elaine realize Charlene means a lot to her, even more than the trains.

In the beginning of the story, Elaine didn't value her relationship with her sister. Elaine felt her little sister Charlene was annoying. She was afraid Charlene would break the trains, and the trains were worth a lot of money. Charlene always wanted to be doing the same things Elaine did. In the story it says Elaine didn't like Charlene hanging around her. Elaine used to shoo Charlene away and yell at her.

When Charlene got hurt by the train table falling on her, Elaine was very worried about Charlene. She knew Charlene was in danger by the way her mother and father were worried. Elaine says she had regrets about how she used to treat Charlene. This made her realize that she valued her sister. When the trains smashed into the wall, Elaine said she didn't even care. She was more worried about her sister.

Sometimes younger sisters and brothers do annoy their older brothers and sisters by hanging around them a lot. Younger sisters and brothers can break things or ask too many questions. You see this a lot in television shows and in real life. Everybody has something they value. They have to think about what are the important things in life to value. For example, what is more important, money or your good health?

In "What Has Value" Elaine learns to value her sister more than she used to value her. The message of the story is to think about what we value and why.

BOOK 3: READING AND WRITING

"Say 'Cheese' "

31. In the chart that follows, identify who influenced the author's interest in photography and how.

Person or People Who Influenced Author	How Person or People Influenced Author
Author's aunt	*Bought her a digital camera to practice shots*

Other possible responses:

Friends—compliment her pictures and say she has a "good eye"

Neighbor—helps her research places that buy photographs and hire photographers

32. Use information from "Say 'Cheese'" to support the opinion that photography makes a good hobby.

The author enjoys photography as a hobby. The reasons for her opinion, according to the story, are that she enjoys it. It is a creative way to express yourself. You can be proud to show and share your work with your friends and family. Sharing photos helps you share memories, too. Finally, you can actually make money with this hobby. You can even earn a living if you are good.

"Music Soothes the Savage Beast"

33. The author says, "At the end of a long day, everyone should have a hobby that will help them relax." How is what the author does in the evening to relax similar to what you might do? How is it different from what you might do? Use details and information from the article to support your comparison.

Sample Response

At the end of a long day, the author says he relaxes with his hobby. His hobby is music. He likes to play the guitar or listen to his CDs. This is similar to what I do sometimes to relax. I don't play the guitar or any other instrument, but I do like to listen to my CDs to relax. Music is important to a lot of my friends, too. We get together and listen to music, too.

34. The authors of "Say 'Cheese'" and "Music Soothes the Savage Beast" both have hobbies they enjoy for different reasons. Write an essay in which you explain which hobby you would prefer and why. Use details from both articles to support your response.

In your response, make sure that you
- tell which hobby you would prefer, photography or music;
- explain why you would prefer that hobby over the other;
- include information and details from both passages to support your response; and
- check your grammar, spelling, and punctuation.

Sample Planning

While your planning page is not graded, take some time to outline the structure of your essay and to plan which information from the stories you will include. You certainly do not have to use a formal outline as demonstrated here, but be sure to plan what you will include in each paragraph. We have used a formal outline structure here to help you visualize the separate paragraphs and contents of each in a very clear way.

I. Introduction
    A. prefer photography
    B. because I like to take photos of my friends
    C. don't want to learn an instrument
II. Supporting details
    A. photography article
        1. capture feelings
        2. have a "good eye"
        3. portfolio of memories
    B. music article
        1. don't have an instrument
        2. prefer quietness
        3. having a "good ear"
III. Going beyond articles
    A. soothes the savage beast
    B. know people who earn money taking photos
IV. Conclusion
    A. prefer photography over music
    B. glad I don't have to make a decision

Sample Response

People enjoy different kinds of hobbies. Some people like fishing. Others like to scrapbook. In "Say 'Cheese'" the writer enjoys photography. In "Music Soothes the Savage Beast" the author likes music. If I had to choose between photography and music as a hobby, I would choose photography. I would like to learn more about taking good pictures so I could take nice pictures of my friends. I really have no interest in playing an instrument, and I don't listen to music very much.

In "Say 'Cheese'" the author says a good photograph captures the feelings or expresses a feeling. I think that is true. I would like to practice photography as a hobby so I could figure out how to take photos that do that. How do you know the right second to snap a picture so you can do that? I think it would be fun to practice taking pictures and learn how to take better pictures. I'd like to show my friends their photos and have them say that I had a "good eye" like the author's friends tell her. I'd like to put together a portfolio, like the author of the article says, too, so I could have an organized collection of all of my photos. It would be like having a journal of memories in pictures.

In "Music Soothes the Savage Beast" the author writes about music as a hobby. I don't have an instrument because I was never really interested in learning how to play one. I prefer quiet times. I rarely listen to music except when someone else turns it on. Like the first author said about having a "good eye" for photography, I don't seem to have a "good ear" for music. I don't sing very well and don't really like to sing.

I've heard the expression "Music soothes the savage beast" before. I have heard that playing music for plants can help them grow better. I'm sure many people like music as a hobby. My friends spend lots of money on CDs and downloading songs from the internet for their iPods. But I also have an uncle who is a professional photographer. He makes a living taking portraits in his studio.

I would prefer photography as a hobby instead of music. I think a lot of it has to do with my not really having a "good ear" for music so I don't enjoy it as much as some people do. The good news, though, is that I really don't have to make a decision or choose between photography or music as a hobby. I could have both as hobbies if I wanted!

Chapter 7

PRACTICE TEST 2

Tips:

To do your best

- carefully read all the directions;
- plan how you will use your time wisely;
- read each question thoroughly; and
- before choosing your response, think about the answer.

BOOK 1: READING

26 Multiple-Choice Questions

55 Minutes to Complete—Work Until You Come to STOP

Each Correct Response Is Worth 1 Point

DIRECTIONS

In Book 1, you will read four or five passages and answer a few questions about each one. Fill in the answers to Book 1 on the bubble sheet on the next page by filling in the letter that matches your answer. Do not write your answers on the test pages. You may make notes or marks on the test pages as you read, though. Be sure to answer all the questions. The correct answers, with explanations, can be found at the end of this chapter.

BOOK 1—ANSWER SHEET

1. Ⓐ Ⓑ Ⓒ Ⓓ   10. Ⓐ Ⓑ Ⓒ Ⓓ   19. Ⓐ Ⓑ Ⓒ Ⓓ

2. Ⓐ Ⓑ Ⓒ Ⓓ   11. Ⓐ Ⓑ Ⓒ Ⓓ   20. Ⓐ Ⓑ Ⓒ Ⓓ

3. Ⓐ Ⓑ Ⓒ Ⓓ   12. Ⓐ Ⓑ Ⓒ Ⓓ   21. Ⓐ Ⓑ Ⓒ Ⓓ

4. Ⓐ Ⓑ Ⓒ Ⓓ   13. Ⓐ Ⓑ Ⓒ Ⓓ   22. Ⓐ Ⓑ Ⓒ Ⓓ

5. Ⓐ Ⓑ Ⓒ Ⓓ   14. Ⓐ Ⓑ Ⓒ Ⓓ   23. Ⓐ Ⓑ Ⓒ Ⓓ

6. Ⓐ Ⓑ Ⓒ Ⓓ   15. Ⓐ Ⓑ Ⓒ Ⓓ   24. Ⓐ Ⓑ Ⓒ Ⓓ

7. Ⓐ Ⓑ Ⓒ Ⓓ   16. Ⓐ Ⓑ Ⓒ Ⓓ   25. Ⓐ Ⓑ Ⓒ Ⓓ

8. Ⓐ Ⓑ Ⓒ Ⓓ   17. Ⓐ Ⓑ Ⓒ Ⓓ   26. Ⓐ Ⓑ Ⓒ Ⓓ

9. Ⓐ Ⓑ Ⓒ Ⓓ   18. Ⓐ Ⓑ Ⓒ Ⓓ

Directions: **Read this poem about a furry ferret friend.
Then answer questions 1 through 6.**

by Ann E. Morris

© Deborah Aronds

1   Hello, my dear daughter.
Just thought you should know.
Your ferret got loose and
Put on quite a show.

5   While you were at school
She unlatched her cage,
Had quite an adventure
Used our house as her stage!

9   When I walked through the door
I had quite a surprise
Your sweet little friend
Tried to don a disguise.

13   But there was no hiding
The damage she'd done
The house was in shambles…LOOK!
But in the long run.

17   She does have cute eyes.
Her temper is sweet
She probably was bored
And needed something to eat.

21
And look at her now

Returned to her bed

She is a bandit,...but

Sweet as cinnamon bread.

1. The best title for this poem would be
   A. "The Naughty-But-Nice Ferret."
   B. "No Place to Run."
   C. "Running Away From Home."
   D. "The Unhappy Ferret."

2. In this poem, the ferret is described as
   A. mean.
   B. thoughtful.
   C. an actress.
   D. scared.

3. The author of this poem is **most likely**
   A. the ferret's owner.
   B. the ferret.
   C. the ferret owner's mother.
   D. the ferret owner's sister.

4. What line from the poem gives the **best** clue that the author was angry?
   A. line 4, "Put on quite a show."
   B. line 10, "I had quite a surprise."
   C. line 12, "Tried to don a disguise."
   D. line 15, "The house was in shambles...LOOK!"

5. The tone of the first four stanzas of this poem is meant to be

   A. annoyed.

   B. suspicious.

   C. scary.

   D. curious.

6. In this poem, line 15, what does the word *shambles* mean?

   A. shaky

   B. orderly

   C. messy

   D. rambling

Go On

Directions: Read the following story and answer questions 7 through 11.

Mayan—from the ancient Maya civilization

gourds—hard-shelled fruit used by some people as cups, bowls, or dippers

stalactite—an icicle-like shape that hangs and is formed from the ceiling of a cave

---

SECRET WATERS OF THE YUCATAN

Alison Black

© aceshot1

The Yucatan is a large peninsula of Mexico bordered by the Gulf of Mexico and the Caribbean Sea. Geographically, it is a flat shelf composed of limestone and coral. This composition acts like a sponge, absorbing rain into the ground. Therefore, few lakes, ponds, or rivers are found in the Yucatan. However, the rainwater collects in underground rivers and stone-lined lakes called cenotes (say-NO-tays). The fresh, clear water of these cenotes, or giant wells, is home to several species of sightless fish that live out their lives in these deep waters.

There are four types of cenotes: completely underground, semiunderground, land level like a lake or pond, and open wells such as the one found at Chichen Itza. The first two types are most common and often located in open fields. The open well at Chichen Itza, one of the finest Mayan ruins of the Yucatan, is a sacred cenote. This natural limestone well provided the city of Chichen Itza its daily water supply. Human bones and precious objects of gold, silver, jade, and copper have also been found in this cenote. Scholars believe it may have been used as a place of sacrifice. In the 1960s an effort was made to explore this deep well. Thousands of gallons of chemicals were poured into it to clarify the waters so objects could be located. Although successful in that many precious objects and skeletons were found and retrieved, the chemicals also destroyed most of the fish and other creatures living in the cenote.

There are over 3,000 cenotes in the Yucatan, but only about half of them have been studied and registered. Cenotes provided water to the ancient people living in the Yucatan. In fact, explorers in the 1800s observed long lines of native people carrying gourds of water from these deep holes.

An outstanding cenote can be found in a small park in the heart of the colonial city of Vallodolid (vayo-DOE-leed). This semi-underground cenote shown in the picture is about 250 feet deep with a walkway all around it. Its caves, stalactites, and hanging vines create a wild, prehistoric atmosphere. Its dark, emerald green waters are also a refreshing surprise as you walk through the city.

The secret waters of the Yucatan are unique and precious. Originally used as a water source, some can now be enjoyed for swimming and cave diving. Many of them, especially the underground or semi-underground cenotes, have very deep, crystal clear waters. These cenotes can only be accessed by rough stone walkways or caves and speak to us of another time and place. They are natural ancient formations, untouched by humans and almost mystical because they are so unique and hidden. You could be in a cenote and easily imagine the "real" world outside as 100 years ago or far removed from Mexico. It is easy to see why cenotes are considered one of the natural wonders of the Yucatan.

7. The **main** purpose of this passage is to
   A. describe the natural wonders of the Yucatan.
   B. persuade tourists to visit the Yucatan Peninsula.
   C. inform the reader about cenotes.
   D. describe the effects of the ancient Mayan civilization on cenotes.

8. According to the story, the fish that live in the cenotes are sightless because
   A. it is dark in the cenotes.
   B. the cenotes have chemicals in them.
   C. they were born that way.
   D. The story does not give a reason why the fish are sightless.

9. What does this phrase from the story **most likely** mean?

   The cenotes **"speak to us of another time and place."**
   A. They remind us of a place where we can get away from things.
   B. We can hear our voices echo when we shout over the cenotes.
   C. Boats can be launched on the cenotes to transport us elsewhere.
   D. Stories have been written about the cenotes in other countries.

10. According to the story, why is rain absorbed into the ground of the Yucatan so readily?

   A. It is surrounded by mountains, so the water becomes trapped.

   B. The limestone and coral composition of the soil soaks up the rain.

   C. The gallons of chemicals clarified the waters.

   D. There are many caves.

11. The author writes

   It is easy to see why cenotes are considered one of the natural wonders of the Yucatan.

   According to the passage, what is one reason why the cenotes are one of the natural wonders of the Yucatan?

   A. They contain limestone.

   B. Gold has been mined from them.

   C. Natural chemicals that kill the fish exist in the water.

   D. They are unique, secret waters.

Go On

Directions: **Read the next passage about sheep. Answer questions 12 through 17.**

> **cast up**—to throw up or regurgitate
>
> **renewable resource**—a natural resource that replenishes or restores itself in time

SHEEP?

Alison Black

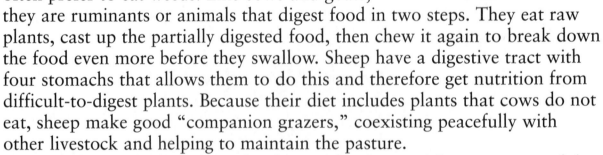

Think about sheep for a moment. What comes to mind? Sheep are usually considered timid, rather unimportant animals. They aren't known for being highly intelligent. Sheep are social animals. They like to be part of a group with other sheep. A group of sheep is called a flock, herd, or mob. Adult females are referred to as ewes, males as rams, and young sheep as lambs.

Sheep are not fussy eaters. They get up to 90 percent of their food from pastureland and often prefer to eat weeds. Like cows and goats, they are ruminants or animals that digest food in two steps. They eat raw plants, cast up the partially digested food, then chew it again to break down the food even more before they swallow. Sheep have a digestive tract with four stomachs that allows them to do this and therefore get nutrition from difficult-to-digest plants. Because their diet includes plants that cows do not eat, sheep make good "companion grazers," coexisting peacefully with other livestock and helping to maintain the pasture.

People have relied on sheep for thousands of years. They were one of the first animals to live with and be of use to humans. As long ago as 6,000 B.C. in what is now the Middle East, shepherds herded sheep. According to the United Nations, more than a billion sheep are raised every year in countries around the world.

Why do people rely on sheep? First, they are raised for their wool. Wool is a renewable resource that can be used in carpets, clothing, and mattresses.

In fact, one sheep can produce as much as 30 pounds of wool annually. Early spinners, weavers, and knitters who worked with sheep's wool discovered that their hands became softer after touching the wool. They learned that a kind of fat called lanolin could be extracted from the wool and used as a softener in soap and other products. Lanolin is an ingredient in many cosmetics.

Furthermore, sheep are important because they are raised for their milk. Their milk is rich in protein and has long been used to make delicious cheeses. Some cheeses traditionally made from sheep's milk include Roquefort, brie, and ricotta.

So the next time you see a "dumb" sheep, consider what it can do and how useful and important it is. Think about nice, wool blankets that keep you warm in the winter, the woolen sweaters you wear, the mattresses you sleep on, or the cheese you eat. Think about hand cream and soap, and thank a sheep.

12. According to the article, why do sheep make good "companion grazers"?

　A. They help guard weaker animals.

　B. They take other animals into their flock.

　C. They are fussy eaters.

　D. They eat weeds and help maintain the pasture.

13. In the sentence

Furthermore, sheep are important because they are raised for their milk.

the word *furthermore* signals to the reader that

　A. sheep are not important.

　B. this is the only reason sheep are useful.

　C. another reason sheep are important came before this reason.

　D. this sentence is based on opinion.

14. Use context clues from paragraph one, what does the author **most likely** mean by this sentence?

    Sheep are social animals.

    A. They prefer to stay in groups.

    B. They communicate with other animals.

    C. They do not like other animals.

    D. They isolate themselves from others.

15. According to this passage, what do cows, goats, and sheep have in common?

    A. They are fussy eaters.

    B. They are ruminants.

    C. They are good companion grazers.

    D. They prefer to eat weeds.

16. Wool is a renewable resource because

    A. it is warm.

    B. it can be woven into many different articles.

    C. it has lanolin in it.

    D. it grows back on sheep and can be cut again.

17. According to the passage, what is one type of cheese that can be made from sheep's milk?

    A. American cheese

    B. Roquefort cheese

    C. Swiss cheese

    D. low-fat cheese

Go On

Directions: **Read this story, then answer questions 18 through 23.**

Brer (pronounced brair)—is a shortened version of Brother.

persimmon—a small, orange-colored, edible fruit that grows on a tree

---

BRER RABBIT AND SISTER COW

Characters: Brer Rabbit, Sister Cow, Brer Rabbit's wife, two of Brer Rabbit's children, Narrator *Setting*: In a pasture of green grass near a dirt road in the country. A briar patch can be seen in the distance. No houses are seen. In the middle of the field, there is a large persimmon tree.

NARRATOR: One sunny day, Brer Rabbit was skipping down the road. He was on his way home to his family that lived in the briar patch. Suddenly, he spotted Sister Cow. She was chewing the grass in the luscious pasture beside the road.

BRER RABBIT: There is Sister Cow. My, some of her milk would taste wonderful on this warm day. I am very thirsty. But I know Sister Cow won't just give me her milk. She has to save it for the farmer. Hmmmm. Let me think.

NARRATOR: So Brer Rabbit thought and thought. Finally, he devised a plan. It was a very clever plan, he thought.

BRER RABBIT (*walking over to Sister Cow*): Why, good day, Sister Cow. And how are you this fine day?

SISTER COW (*lifting her head from the grass*): I'm just fine, Brer Rabbit. How are you and your family these days?

BRER RABBIT: We're mighty fine, Sister Cow. Thanks for asking. But I need some help. Can you help me?

SISTER COW: Well, that depends. What do you need?

BRER RABBIT: I'd like to bring some tasty persimmons home to my family. There are some way up in that tree right there, but I cannot reach them. (*points to persimmon tree*) If you can just knock the tree with your head a few times, maybe enough persimmons for both of us to bring home to our families will fall.

NARRATOR: Sister Cow considered this idea. Then, thinking how much her family would enjoy the tasty fruit, she took a running start toward the tree. She tipped her horns down and butted her head against the persimmon tree as hard as she could. Her horns got stuck in the tree trunk.

SISTER COW: Help me, Brer Rabbit. My horns are stuck (*trying to yank her horns out*).

BRER RABBIT: I'll need help. I'll run home and bring my family.

NARRATOR: Brer Rabbit did run home. He returned with his family and a big pail. They milked Sister Cow, draining every last drop of milk while her horns were firmly stuck in the tree.

SISTER COW: You tricked me, Brer Rabbit. This was your plan all along (*still pulling and tugging to free herself*).

BRER RABBIT: Thank you, Sister Cow. We'll return tomorrow for more milk since I'm sure you'll be stuck here until your farmer comes looking to milk you in the morning.

NARRATOR: Rabbit's family left with their pail of milk, leaving Sister Cow trapped in the tree. Sister Cow struggled and struggled to free her horns. She finally freed herself.

SISTER COW: That Brer Rabbit. He'll pay for this. I have tricks of my own!

NARRATOR: The next day when Sister Cow saw Brer Rabbit in the distance, she stuck her horns back into the holes in the tree trunk pretending to still be stuck. What Sister Cow didn't know was that Brer Rabbit had very good eyes. Better than hers. He had seen Sister Cow grazing from the distance. He knew she was free from the tree.

BRER RABBIT (*chuckling quietly to himself*): What trick does she have up her sleeve? I'll play along and see what she's up to.

NARRATOR: When he got nearer, he said to Sister Cow...

BRER RABBIT: How are you today, Sister Cow?

SISTER COW: I'm feeling poorly. Can you please pull me out? Reach behind me and pull my tail. Get me out.

BRER RABBIT: And have you trample me? No, no, no. This is as close as I plan to get!

SISTER COW (*furious that her plan hadn't worked*): You are infuriating, Brer Rabbit!

NARRATOR: With that, she yanked her horns around and chased Brer Rabbit all the way to the briar patch. But when she gave up—because cows don't like the prickly nature of a briar patch—Brer Rabbit relaxed and enjoyed a nice, long drink of Sister Cow's milk from the day before.

18. What is the **main** conflict in this story?

   A. Brer Rabbit traps Sister Cow; Sister Cow wants to escape.

   B. Brer Rabbit wants milk; Sister Cow wants persimmons.

   C. Brer Rabbit tricks Sister Cow; Sister Cow tricks Brer Rabbit.

   D. Brer Rabbit milks Sister Cow; Brer Rabbit chases Sister Cow.

19. According to the story, why did Brer Rabbit trick Sister Cow?

   A. He knew she wouldn't just give him the milk that he wanted.

   B. She had tricked him the day before.

   C. He was angry with her.

   D. His family was very hungry and needed the persimmons to survive.

20. According to the story, Brer Rabbit can be **best** described as

    A. tender.

    B. angry.

    C. devious.

    D. lazy.

21. Which of these statements **best** identifies the way this story is organized?

    A. Hyperlinks are provided to additional information.

    B. Events are organized in the order in which they occurred.

    C. There is a cause-and-effect organization.

    D. There is a compare-and-contrast organization.

22. For what reason does Sister Cow **most likely** try to trick Brer Rabbit?

    A. She had nothing else to do.

    B. He had hurt her horns.

    C. She was hungry.

    D. She wanted revenge.

23. What genre of writing does this passage **most** resemble?

    A. a newspaper article

    B. a report

    C. a poem

    D. a play

Go On

Directions: **Finally, read this passage and answer questions 24 through 26.**

CAN I REALLY LOOK LIKE HER?

Jill Lassonde

© Anatoliy Babiychuk

The magazine ad says this makeup will
make me beautiful and flawless.

I have to buy it.

The model in the picture is indeed both
beautiful and without flaws.

I use it, but I still don't look like Her!

The TV commercial shows a beautiful woman with
a tan that glistens and radiates.

This tanning lotion is unlike any other.

There is no fake orange color, only beautiful bronzed color.

I use it, but I still don't look like Her!

The fitness instructor swears by her workout plan.

It is the only way to get fit like she is.

I go out to buy her DVD.

I use it, but I still don't look like Her!

Ooooh, look!! A new diet drink!
And this one is absolutely guaranteed to work!

I have to buy it!

Maybe then I'll look like Her.

But then I think…wait a minute! What's so wrong with Me?

24. Throughout this poem, why does the author Jill **most likely** capitalize the word "Her"?

 A. The author doesn't know the model's name so she just names her.

 B. "Her" is the model's name.

 C. "Her" symbolizes the ideal person the author wants to look like.

 D. She made an error in capitalizing it.

25. What is the idea or message the author of this poem **most likely** wants to tell the reader?

 A. The models in ads are not real people.

 B. Be happy with who you are.

 C. We should never listen to advertisements.

 D. Advertisements are always untrustworthy.

26. According to the poem, which products worked **best** for Jill?

   A. the tanning lotion

   B. the exercise DVD

   C. the diet drink

   D. The poem does not indicate which product worked best, if at all.

STOP

BOOK 2: LISTENING AND WRITING

3 Short Responses and 1 Extended Response

60 Minutes to Complete *After* Passage Is Read Twice

Book 2 Responses Are Worth a Total of 5 Points

DIRECTIONS

Book 2 asks you to write about a passage that will be read to you. When you write your responses, DO NOT write about your personal opinions. However, you should make connections beyond the reading in the final essay response (question 30). Before you begin this practice test, it is recommended that you review the scoring rubric in Appendix C to guide your writing. Your responses will be scored based on the following:

- Have you clearly organized your ideas?
- Have you clearly expressed your ideas?
- Have you completely and accurately answered the questions?
- Have you supported the ideas in your responses by examples from the passage?
- Is your writing enjoyable and interesting to the reader?
- Have you used accurate grammar, spelling, punctuation, and paragraphing?

In Book 2 in this practice test, you will listen to a story called "Memories of My Father of Perfection" by Melissa Lounsbury. Then, you will read the questions in this part of the test and write your answers to show you understood the story.

The story will be read to you not once, but twice. Listen carefully and take notes on the story. Use your notes to answer the following questions about the story.

When you have completed your answers, use the rubrics in Appendix C to score your responses. Then, read the sample responses at the end of this chapter and use this model and the rubric to revise and improve your responses and score.

Note to Reader: Read the entire passage two times from beginning to end. Start with the title and author each time. Read at a comfortable pace.

MEMORIES OF MY FATHER OF PERFECTION

Melissa Lounsbury

I was three years old, and it was Father's Day. My preschool was having a Father's Day party. All of my preschool friends had invited their fathers to the party, as well as other family members. My father came, too.

During the party, my teacher called all of the children up on stage. In our two-story nursery school building, there was a small wooden stage about two feet off the ground. A soft, velvet red curtain draped the stage. It was a very special place to be. It made me feel like a famous movie star to stand up there and look down at everyone who was looking up at me. My friends and I waited patiently to see what was going to happen next. Then my teacher asked the fathers to join us. My dad came up on stage and stood next to me. I felt as tall as him that day. I was so proud that everyone could see my dad standing right next to me up on that stage. It seemed life couldn't get any better than this. It was like a dream.

Next, the teacher had us play a game with our fathers on the stage. She directed our fathers to close their eyes while all of us children put our shoes into a big basket. Our fathers were to go into the container and find which shoes were ours. As a three year old, I thought this was the coolest game. As soon as the teacher said "Go!" my father rushed over to the pool-sized basket and within less than a minute had found my shiny, ruby red shoes. My family called them my "Dorothy shoes" because we had watched "The Wizard of Oz" together. My father bent his knees and snatched my shoes out of the basket as quick as a rabbit. He rushed back to where I was standing so tall and proud. When he bowed down to put my shoes on my tiny feet, I felt like Cinderella. Of course, the shoe was a perfect fit. I embraced him as tightly as I could. I was so proud that my father knew exactly which shoes were mine. I felt very close to him because he really knew and loved me!

Memories are powerful links to our past. As I sit here and think back on the memories I have of my life, the ones of my father are the most precious to me. As I mature into a young adult, I think about where I've been, where I am, where I'm going, and how much my father has had an influence on every moment of my life. He has been my guiding force, and I hope he always will be. Life has taught me that nothing lasts forever except the memories we create. I look forward to every new memory I create with my father. He is, by far, my Father of Perfection.

NOTES

NOTES

STOP

*Start Timing the 60 Minutes
After the Passage Has Been Read Twice.*

27. Complete the chart that follows by describing, according to the story, how Melissa feels about her father and one reason why she feels this way.

How Melissa Feels About Her Father	One Reason Why She Feels This Way

© Melanie DeFazio

28. The author describes the stage where the Father's Day event took place. How does the stage setting make Melissa feel? Use details from the story to support your response.

_____

_____

_____

_____

_____

_____

_____

_____

29. Melissa refers to her father as her "Father of
Perfection." Using information from the story,
describe why she calls him this.

_____

_____

_____

_____

_____

_____

_____

Go On

PLANNING PAGE

PLAN your writing for question 30 on this page. DO NOT write your final essay here, however. Whatever you write on this page WILL NOT be scored as your final response. Write your final essay response on the lines on the next pages.

30. The author Melissa writes

Life has taught me that nothing lasts forever except the memories we create.

What memories has Melissa created with her father? How do we know that Melissa treasures her memories of her father? Use information from the passage to support your response.

In your response, make sure that you

■ describe what memories Melissa has created with her father;

■ describe how we know Melissa treasures her memories of her father;

■ include information and details from the passage to support your response; and

■ check your grammar, spelling, and punctuation.

_____

_____

_____

_____

_____

_____

_____

_____

_____

Go On

_____

_____

_____

_____

_____

_____

_____

_____

_____

_____

_____

_____

_____

_____

_____

_____

_____

STOP

BOOK 3: READING AND WRITING

3 Short Responses and 1 Extended Response

60 Minutes

Book 3 Responses Are Worth a Total of 5 Points

DIRECTIONS

Book 3 asks you to write about two passages that you read. When you write your responses, DO NOT write about your personal opinions. Your responses will be scored based on the following:

- Have you clearly organized your ideas?
- Have you clearly expressed your ideas?
- Have you completely and accurately answered the questions?
- Have you supported the ideas in your responses by examples from the passage?
- Is your writing enjoyable and interesting to the reader?
- Have you used accurate grammar, spelling, punctuation, and paragraphing?

In Book 3 you will read two passages. One is called "Going to School in India" and is written by Anuradhaa from an interview with Shradha Sane, a student in India. The other passage is called "A Day in a Chinese Bilingual Elementary School" by Hanfu Mi. Use what you read in the passages to answer questions 31 through 34. You may look back and reread the passages any time you want to while answering the questions. Sample responses can be found at the end of this chapter.

GOING TO SCHOOL IN INDIA

Anuradhaa Shastri
(Pronounced ah-noo-RAH-dah SHAS-three)

Following is a story written by Anuradhaa based on a telephone interview from New York with Ms. Shradha (SHRAH-dah) Sane (SAH-nay), who is presently a seventh-grader at Ahilya (ah-HIL-ya) Devi (DAY-vee) High School for Girls in Poona, India. Anuradhaa wishes to thank Shradha.

tsunami (soo-NAH-mee)—gigantic sea wave created when undersea volcanoes erupt

Hello, everyone! I am in sixth grade and studying in India. I thought I would share with you some of my experiences at school.

Ours is an all-girls high school from grades five through ten. Our school year begins in the month of June and ends in April. We have a three week school break during Diwali, our festival of lights. Diwali is celebrated around late October or early November.

From Monday through Friday our school timings are from noon to 5:30 p.m. On Saturdays we go from 7:10 a.m. to 11:30 a.m. Every day, unfortunately, we have to wear a school uniform. This is a white blouse, a green jumper dress, white socks, and sneakers. During the winter months, we wear a green sweater, too. Girls with short hair have to wear a black hair band. Those with long hair should have two braids tied in black ribbons.

Each grade has six sections. Sections A, B, and C are called Semi-English sections. This is because math and science subjects are taught in English. These sections also have English language as one subject. The rest of the subjects are taught in Marathi, which is the regional language of our state. In the remaining three sections—D, E, and F—all the subjects are taught in Marathi. There are about 60 students in each section.

I enjoy our morning routine. We begin by singing the National Anthem. This is followed by a Pledge and then a prayer. While the prayer is being recited on the mike (microphone), we do our deep-breathing exercises.

Morning routine is followed by the first period, which is usually science. The other subjects we study are math, history, geography, Hindi language, English language, computer, drawing, music, and physical training. My drawing teacher is very strict. She gives us difficult topics to draw, and I don't know how to draw very well. This is not a class I really enjoy. Our school playground is very small, and I wish we had more room to play in a large group. My math teacher is very good, though. I like her a lot. She explains very well, and I enjoy her class. I also love our Sports Day. We have different games and folk dances. We also have projects per term. We did a group project on water pollution. Right now, I am working on an individual project on tsunamis. I am learning lots of interesting facts about them. We have homework every day. It takes me about an hour and a half to complete after school. As you can see, the day is very busy.

Hope you can visit my school some day! You may borrow one of my uniforms to wear, if you would like.

31. In the chart that follows, identify two routines Shradha likes about her school day in India and two she does *not* like.

What Shradha Likes About School	What Shradha Does *Not* Like About School
1.	1.
2.	2.

32. How is Shradha's school experience like your typical day in school? Use details from the story in your response.

_____

_____

_____

_____

_____

_____

_____

Go On

bilingual—two languages are taught, spoken, or used

A DAY IN A CHINESE BILINGUAL ELEMENTARY SCHOOL

Hanfu Mi

My name is Guo Wenxuan (GYOO WENS-joo-on), but all my friends call me Xixi (SEE-see). I am a 10-year-old Chinese girl, attending the fourth grade in a bilingual elementary school in the capital city of a northern province in China. Unlike many children of my age, I go to this private boarding school. There are 7 classes at my grade with about 38 students in each class. In my class, there are 20 boys and 18 girls. My homeroom teacher is a female. More than 90 percent of the teachers at my school are female. Every week, I stay at school for five days and go home on the weekend with a lot of homework. Other than more emphasis on English, my school is like most of the other schools in the city. I have a 1-month winter vacation and a 1.5-month summer vacation. Although during both vacations I do not have to wear my school uniform, I still have to do a lot of homework.

At 6:10, I get up and start my school day. The morning self-study session begins at 6:45 and lasts until 7:30. Then, I have 30 minutes to eat my breakfast. Classes start at 8:00. There are 4 periods in the morning and 3 periods in the afternoon. They are 40 minutes each. There is a 10-minute break between classes. After the second period, all the students have to jog in the winter and do morning exercises in the summer. Then, we do eye exercises. I do not like jogging nor doing the eye exercises. I especially dislike all the quizzes and tests, which are too frequent at my school. I enjoy taking the computer class and hearing the class dismissal bell ring every time. I take Chinese, mathematics, English, character education and society, science, computer, and physical education almost daily. I also have to attend a class meeting every day. Twice a week, I take music class and art class. I have lunch at 11:30. Afterwards, the noon self-study session starts at 12:20 and runs until 1:00 in the afternoon. I take a nap from 1:00 till 2:00. At 2:10, the fifth period starts. The free period is between 4:30 and 5:30. The evening self-study session lasts one hour from 5:30 till 6:30. Supper starts at 7:00. We all have to attend the evening reading session between 8:10 and 9:00. At 9:30, I finish with my school day and go to bed.

33. Which customs and activities that the author Hanfu Mi describes in "A Day in a Chinese Bilingual Elementary School" would you like to include in your school day? Why? Which would you *not* want to include? Why? Use details and information from the article to support your response.

_____

_____

_____

_____

_____

_____

_____

Go On

PLANNING PAGE

PLAN your writing for question 34 on this page. DO NOT write your final essay here, however. Whatever you write on this page WILL NOT be scored as your final response. Write your final essay response on the lines on the next pages.

34. The authors of "Going to School in India" and "A Day in a Chinese Bilingual Elementary School" write about children who attend schools in countries outside the United States. Using details from Anuradhaa's and Hanfu's stories, compare what customs and activities are similar between the two schools. Then, describe how the two school experiences contrast or are different from each other. Write an essay in which you compare and contrast the two school experiences. Use details from both stories.

In your response, make sure that you

- compare the similarities between the two school experiences;
- contrast the differences between the two school experiences;
- use details from both stories to support your response; and
- check your grammar, spelling, and punctuation.

_____

_____

_____

_____

_____

_____

_____

Go On

_____

_____

_____

_____

_____

_____

_____

_____

_____

_____

_____

_____

_____

_____

_____

_____

_____

_____

_____

STOP

ANSWERS AND EXPLANATIONS

BOOK 1: READING

About a Ferret Poem

1. **A** This response represents the whole poem, whereas the other choices represent only parts.

2. **C** The poem describes her putting on a show and being on stage like an actress.

3. **C** The first stanza refers to the author's "dear daughter."

4. **D** The tone is angry because the author says the house is in shambles and uses all capital letters and an exclamation mark for LOOK! This implies anger.

5. **A** These stanzas show annoyance because the author is telling about how the ferret did bad things.

6. **C** Use context clues. The previous line says damage was done to the house.

"Secret Waters of the Yucatan"

7. **C** This passage informs. It does not persuade, talk about other natural wonders besides the cenotes, or talk about the effects of the Mayans.

8. **D** While we are told the fish are sightless, the article does not give a reason why.

9. **A** The cenotes remind us of places to go to escape.

10. **B** The soil composition absorbs like a sponge.

11. **D** The story does not state any of the other choices.

"Sheep?"

12. **D** The story does not state any of the other choices.

13. **C** "Furthermore" is a transition word that implies a connection between what came before and what follows.

14. **A** Sheep prefer to stay in groups because they are social animals.

15. **B** The story does not state any of the other choices.

16. **D** A renewable resource is one that grows back. Sheep's wool grows back.

17. **B** Roquefort is listed in the passage. The other choices are not.

"Brer Rabbit and Sister Cow"

18. **A** The main conflict is that the cow gets trapped and escapes.

19. **A** The story says Brer Rabbit knew Sister Cow wouldn't just give him her milk.

20. **C** Items A, B, and D should be eliminated because the story does not support these characteristics. He is devious because he tricks the cow.

21. **B** Events are sequenced by what happened first, next, then next, and so on.

22. **D** Sister Cow says "He'll pay for this." This indicates revenge.

23. **D** The format reflects a play. The characters and setting are given, then the characters' lines.

"Can I Really Look Like Her?"

24. **C** "Her" is a symbol of who Jill wants to be.

25. **B** The last line of the poem supports choice B.

26. **D** The poem gives no evidence any of the products worked for Jill.

BOOK 2: LISTENING AND WRITING

"Memories of My Father of Perfection"

27. Complete the chart that follows by describing, according to the story, how Melissa feels about her father and one reason why she feels this way.

How Melissa Feels About Her Father	One Reason Why She Feels This Way
Proud	*Because he really knew and loved her*

Other possible answers:

Proud — because he had found her shoes in the basket so quickly

Love — he has been her guiding force

Proud — she sees him as her Father of Perfection

28. The author describes the stage where the Father's Day event took place. How does the stage setting make Melissa feel? Use details from the story to support your response.

Sample Response

Melissa says the stage makes her feel "like a famous movie star." She describes the soft, velvet curtain that is draped on the stage and says it was a very special place to be. She also felt very proud to be standing on the stage with her father. She says she felt as tall as him that day.

29. Melissa refers to her father as her "Father of Perfection." Using information from the story, describe why she calls him this.

Sample Response

Melissa's father is her "Father of Perfection" because she was proud of him and had powerful memories of him. Not only did he find her shoes so quickly on Father's Day and stand next to her on the special stage, but throughout her life he has had an influence on everything she has done. In her eyes he has been a perfect guiding force who has helped her in every moment of her life. It sounds like he has always been there when she needed him and that makes him perfect to her. He is reliable.

30. The author Melissa writes

Life has taught me that nothing lasts forever except the memories we create.

What memories has Melissa created with her father? How do we know that Melissa treasures her memories of her father? Use information from the passage to support your response.

In your response, make sure that you
- describe what memories Melissa has created with her father;
- describe how we know Melissa treasures her memories of her father;
- include information and details from the passage to support your response; and
- check your grammar, spelling, and punctuation.

Sample Planning Page

While your planning page is not graded, take some time to outline the structgure of your essay and to plan which information from the story you will include. You certainly do not have to use a formal outline as demonstrated here, but be sure to plan what you will include in each paragraph. We have used a formal outline structure here to help you visualize the paragraphs and contents of each in a very clear way.

I. Introduction
    A. repeat quoted sentence from story
    B. story gives us proof
II. Supporting details
    A. memories Melissa has created with her father
        1. Father's Day event and shoes
        2. influence her father has had in her life
    B. how we know she treasures these memories
        1. this story shows her pride
        2. says how powerful and precious memories are
III. Connections
    A. people keep photographs and journals
    B. personal memories of my father
IV. Conclusion

Sample Response

In her story "Memories of My Father of Perfection," the author Melissa Lounsbury writes that "Life has taught me that nothing lasts forever except the memories we create." Melissa has powerful memories of her father. We know she treasures these memories by what she writes in this essay.

Melissa has not only created a lot of memories with her father, but she hopes to continue to create more. This story is a memory of a Father's Day party that took place when Melissa was three years old at her preschool. She describes how proud she was when her father found her shoes. She also tells how he called them her "Dorothy shoes" because they had watched "The Wizard of Oz" together. So that is another good memory she has. In the last paragraph, she also writes that the memories of her father are most precious to her. Her father has had a big influence on her life, so she must have created many good memories with him by doing lots of things together.

We know Melissa treasures these moments with her father because, first of all, she chose to write this essay about him and how proud she is of him. That's an honor right there. In her story, she talks about being proud. She writes things like "I embraced him as tightly as I could" to show how dear a memory this is for her.

Many people have memories that they try to keep alive forever because they are special. Proof of this is that people keep souvenirs and photographs and talk about their memories with friends and family. When my family gets together, we always bring out pictures. We share the memories we have of my father, too.

Melissa's story is proof that she believes that memories do last forever. She treasures the memories she has and plans to continue to create memories with her father.

BOOK 3: READING AND WRITING

"Going to School in India"

31. In the chart that follows, identify two routines Shradha likes about her school day in India and two she does *not* like.

What Shradha Likes About School	What Shradha Does *Not* Like About School
1. *Morning routine*	1. *Wearing a school uniform*
2. *Sports Day*	2. *Drawing class*

Other possible responses:

Likes—singing National Anthem, the Pledge, the prayer, deep-breathing exercises, her math teacher, that her math teacher explains well, the games and folk dances during Sports Day

Does Not Like—the small playground; that she cannot play in large groups on the playground

32. How is Shradha's school experience like your typical day in school? Use details from the story in your response.

Sample Response

Shradha's day in a school in India is like my typical day in school in many ways. In both schools, we take different subjects. We both take math, science, computers, art, music, and gym. In the story the author calls gym "physical training" and calls art class "drawing." Both schools have

playgrounds, too. Shradha says their playground is small. We both have morning routines, too. In India they say the Pledge, and we do, too. I'm sure we don't say the same Pledge, though. Finally, both schools give homework. Shradha's homework usually takes her about an hour and a half. That's about how long my homework takes me, too.

"A Day in a Chinese Bilingual Elementary School"

33. Which customs and activities Xixi describes in "A Day in a Chinese Bilingual Elementary School" would you like to include in your school day? Why? Which would you *not* want to include? Why? Use details and information from the article to support your response.

Sample Response

I would like to include some of the customs and activities described in this passage in my school day. I would like to see what it is like to do the eye exercises, even though Xixi says she doesn't like them. I also would like to live at school during the week and go home on the weekends. It would be fun to live with your school friends during the week. I would like to learn to speak Chinese, too.

On the other hand, there are some customs and activities I would not want to include in my day. Xixi's school day and school year are much longer than mine. They start the day at 6:10 a.m. and end at 9:30 P.M. They don't seem to have much free time. Every hour is scheduled for them. There is lots of homework, according to Xixi. They even have to do homework during their breaks. Seems like everyone has tests and quizzes, too. There's no getting away from them!

34. The authors of "Going to School in India" and "A Day in a Chinese Bilingual Elementary School" write about children who attend schools in countries outside the United States. Using details from Anuradhaa's and Hanfu's stories, compare what customs and activities are similar between the two schools. Then, describe how the two school experiences contrast or differ from each other. Write an essay in which you compare and contrast the two school experiences. Use details from both stories.

In your response, make sure that you

■ compare the similarities between the two school experiences;

■ contrast the differences between the two school experiences;

■ use details from both stories to support your response; and

■ check your grammar, spelling, and punctuation.

Sample Planning

While your planning page is not graded, take some time to outline the structure of your essay and to plan which information from the stories you will include. You certainly do not have to use a formal outline as demonstrated here but be sure to plan what you will include in each paragraph. We have used a formal outline structure here to help you visualize the separate paragraphs and contents of each in a very clear way.

I. *Introduction*

    A. *stories tell about school in India and China*

    B. *characteristics of their days*

    C. *there are similarities and differences*

II. Supporting details

    A. similarities

        1. similar courses

        2. uniforms

        3. homework

        4. morning routines

    B. Differences

        1. where students live

        2. number of students in class

        3. English used

        4. boys/girls

        5. morning routines

III. Going beyond articles

    A. how kids are similar around the world

    B. homework and uniforms

IV. Conclusion

    A. interesting to learn about India and China

    B. schools in other countries

Sample Response

    The two passages tell about schools in two different countries: China and India. Shradha, a student in India, and Xixi, a student in China, tell what it is like to be students, what they like and don't like, and what their schedules are. By reading these two stories, we get an idea of how the two schools they go to are similar and different.

    In India and China, these students take similar courses. They learn math, science, computers, music, and art. Both students have to wear uniforms to school. Also, they both tell about having homework to do after school. Finally, both schools have morning routines to start their days. Both do morning exercises.

The students have different experiences, too, though. For example, Xixi's school is a private boarding school. She lives at the school Mondays through Fridays and goes home on the weekends. Shradha lives at home and goes to school Monday through Saturday. In Shradha's class there are 60 students. That is a large-sized class. She has only girls in her class. Xixi's class size is 38 students, and it is mixed with boys and girls. In both schools the English language is used, but in India some classes are taught in English. For example, Shradha's math and science classes are taught in English. In China they have a class where they learn to speak English. Finally, while both schools have morning routines, these routines are different. In China students jog, exercise, and do eye exercises. In India students do deep breathing exercises, say the Pledge, sing, and pray.

While reading these passages, I couldn't help but think how students are similar all around the world. We all seem to like and dislike the same things. We like being with our friends, playing, working with good teachers, and learning about interesting things. But we also dislike homework and wearing school uniforms. I have heard and read about schools in other cultures besides China and India. While schools may be different, children seem to be very similar in what they like and dislike about school.

It was interesting to learn about schools and being a student in India and China by reading these passages. The world is a big place, but maybe the people in it aren't so different after all.

LITERARY GENRES

autobiography—The true story of a person's life written by the person.

biography—The true story of a person's life.

diary or journal—Dated, personal entries of the writer's feelings, thoughts, and telling of events. We can learn about history by reading journals of people who lived during those times.

fable—A story that teaches a lesson or has a moral. Usually its characters are animals, nonhuman objects, or forces of nature that are given human qualities. *The Tortoise and the Hare* is a popular example of a fable.

fairy tale—A pretend story that features magical, enchanted characters, such as fairies, elves, witches, giants, or talking animals. We usually think of fairy tales as beginning with "Once upon a time..." and ending with "...and they lived happily ever after." *Shrek* and *Cinderella* are fairy tales.

fantasy—A pretend story that takes place in an imaginary, magical world of its own. This world may have its own rules, language, and culture. *The Lord of the Rings* is an example of a fantasy that takes place in a fantasy world.

historical fiction—A story that is based on a real event, person, or circumstance in the past but is fictional (did not happen in exactly the same way as told). *The Last of the Mohicans* and the American Girl® series are examples of historical fiction.

mystery—A story whose plot revolves around finding a solution to a crime or a who-done-it situation. Nate the Great and Sherlock Holmes were always solving mysteries.

myth—A story that uses the supernatural to explain natural events. Myths are linked to the spiritual life of a community. There are many myths of Greek gods and goddesses, such as Zeus.

science fiction—A story that takes place in the future, involves speculations based on current technology and science, and usually goes beyond what can really happen in nature. Stories about time travel and outer space aliens are sci-fi.

tall tale—A humorously exaggerated story that explains a natural phenomenon. For example, the giant footsteps of the lumberjack Paul Bunyan and his blue ox, Babe, formed Minnesota's ten thousand lakes. Bunyan also dug the Grand Canyon by dragging his big ax behind him.

GLOSSARY OF TERMS

alliteration—Tongue twisters that repeat beginning sounds. Example: Sue *sells* *sea*shells.

cause and effect—One event is a consequence of the other. The first event is the cause; the second is the result.

characters—People, or sometimes animals, that are portrayed in a book or movie.

compare—To describe the similarities among two or more events, characters, and so on.

conflict—The problem or struggle in a story.

context clues—Little suggestions that help readers figure out the meaning of an unfamiliar word by using the meaning of the other words in the sentence or paragraph.

contrast—To describe the differences among two or more events, characters, and so on.

essay—A nonfiction piece that focuses on a topic.

fact—Something that can be proven.

fiction—An imaginary story.

genre—A category of types of writing or reading. Examples: essays, formal letters, poetry, and fiction.

graphic organizer—A visual representation of how details are related or connected to each other. Examples: a t-chart, a Venn diagram.

imagery—Words and phrases that come from the five senses.

main idea—The primary point the author makes in the piece.

metaphor—When two things that are unalike but may have one thing in common are compared without using the word *like* or *as* in the comparison. Example: The river was a lazy snail.

motivation—A character's reason for acting, thinking, or feeling a certain way.

narrative—Any piece that tells a story.

nonfiction—Tells a story that really happened.

onomatopoeia—Using words that sound like what they mean. Example: Hiss, bang, and whack.

opinion—Something that a person believes to be true but cannot be proven as a fact.

personification—Giving animals or inanimate objects human characteristics. Example: talking dogs.

plot—Related, sequenced events that make up a story.

rubric—An assessment tool used to measure progress or achievement.

setting—The physical place and time in which a story takes place.

simile—When two things that are unalike but may have one thing in common are compared using the word *like* or *as* in the comparison. Example: She was as quiet as a mouse.

stanza—Like a paragraph in an essay, a stanza in a poem is a grouping of two or more lines.

summarize—Pulling together the important ideas in a piece and stating them in your own words.

t-chart—A graphic or visual representation of information that is set in columns with headings for each category.

theme—An idea that is repeated throughout a piece.

voice—A writer's style of expression.

web—A graphic or visual representation of information displayed with circles and lines that are interconnected in a way to show the relationships between each idea or event.

SAMPLE SCORING RUBRICS*

GRADE 6 ENGLISH LANGUAGE ARTS RUBRIC CHART

(Used for scoring Book 2: Listening/Writing, questions 27 through 30, then Book 3: Reading/Writing, questions 31 through 34. Read the responses in each book as a whole and score them together as a cluster. Questions 27 through 30 will be given one score from 0 to 5. Then, questions 31 through 34 will be given one score from 0 to 5.)

GRADE 6 WRITING MECHANICS RUBRIC CHART

(Used for scoring Book 2: Listening/Writing, question 30, and Book 3: Reading/Writing, question 34, as a whole. Read the responses to both of these questions, and then score them together as either 0, 1, 2, or 3. Note: There is one score for both responses assessed together.)

---

*The New York State scoring rubrics used to score the short- and extended-response questions in Books 2 and 3 may be found online at *http://www.emsc.nysed.gov/3-8/ela-sample/gr6-sg.pdf*.

GRADE 6 ENGLISH LANGUAGE ARTS RUBRIC CHART

Quality	Responses earning a score of 5	Responses earning a score of 4
Meaning: Do the responses show the reader understood the task and the passage(s)?	As a whole, do responses 1. answer the question? 2. address the theme? 3. thoroughly interpret the passage(s)? 4. go beyond the passage(s)?	As a whole, do the responses 1. answer part of the question? 2. address key elements of the passage(s)? 3. interpret the passage(s) at a literal or surface level? 4. go beyond the passage(s)?
Development: Are the ideas elaborated and is information from the passage(s) used to support the responses?	As a whole, do responses 1. elaborate and develop ideas fully? 2. use relevant details and examples from the passage(s)?	As a whole, do responses 1. answer the questions but elaborate only a little? 2. use some examples from the passage(s)? 3. perhaps include some minor inaccuracies?
Organization: Are the written responses coherent and do they have good focus and structure?	Do the extended responses 1. have and maintain a clear focus? 2. show a logical progression of ideas in an organized way?	Do the extended responses 1. have a general focus but perhaps contain some irrelevant details? 2. show clear organization is attempted?
Language Use: Do the responses show an awareness of who the reader will be and use effective words, sentence variety, and sentence structure for this type of reader?	Do the extended responses 1. sound interesting and read smoothly? 2. use a variety of sentence structures and some advanced vocabulary?	Do the extended responses 1. sound somewhat interesting and are they readable? 2. use mostly simple sentences and basic vocabulary?

Responses earning a score of 3	Responses earning a score of 2	Responses earning a score of 1
As a whole, do the responses 1. answer part of the questions? 2. address a few key elements of the passage(s)? 3. show the reader might not have understood parts of the passage(s)? 4. go beyond the passage(s)?	As a whole, do the responses 1. answer part of the question? 2. address basic elements of the theme? 3. demonstrate the reader only understood parts of the passage(s)? 4. only make slight connections beyond the passage(s)?	As a whole, do the responses 1. answer very few of the questions? 2. address few elements of the passage(s)? 3. demonstrate the reader only understood parts of the passage(s)? 4. make few or no connections beyond the passage(s)?
As a whole, do the responses 1. answer questions only briefly? 2. use only a few examples from the passage(s)? 3. maybe include some minor inaccuracies?	As a whole, do the responses 1. use just a couple of examples from the passage(s)? 2. refer to some details from the passage(s) inaccurately?	As a whole, do the responses 1. use almost no examples from the passage(s)? 2. maybe include inaccuracies?
Do the extended responses 1. try to maintain a focus but go off course here and there? 2. attempt organization?	Do the extended responses 1. try to maintain a focus? 2. include irrelevant information 3. show little organization or attempt to organize?	Do the extended responses 1. lack any focus? 2. repeat information or focus on unimportant information? 3. show little organization or attempt to organize?
Do the extended responses 1. sound somewhat interesting and are they readable? 2. use mostly simple sentences and basic vocabulary?	Do not extended responses 1. sound somewhat interesting and are they readable? 2. keep repeating same basic vocabulary? 3. use disconnected ideas and pieces of thoughts?	Do not extended responses 1. appear hard to read? 2. use simple vocabulary? 3. include disconnected ideas and pieces of thoughts?

A score of 0 means the responses were not correct, not relevant, or not comprehendible.

GRADE 6 WRITING MECHANICS RUBRIC CHART

Quality	Responses earning a score of 3	Response`s earning a score of 2	Responses earning a score of 1
Conventions: Do the responses represent accurate • spelling, • grammar, • punctuation, • capitalization, paragraphing, and • language use?	Do the written responses represent that the writer has control of English writing conventions?	Do the written responses represent that the writer has partial control of English writing conventions?	Do the written responses represent that the writer has minimal control of English writing conventions?
	Are spelling errors minor or repeated? Do spelling errors occur mainly in advanced vocabulary?	Do the few errors slightly interfere only with reading and understanding the responses?	Do errors in conventions interfere with the reader's ability to generally read and understand the responses?
	Are other conventions largely accurate?	Are there only a few errors in conventions?	Are there frequent errors in conventions?

A score of 0 means the written responses represent the writer has no control over the English writing conventions. Abundant errors make the responses incomprehensible.

INDEX